"This book is not for Crybabies"

FOG CITY
DINER®
COOKBOOK

BY CINDY PAWLCYN

TEN SPEED PRESS

Ten Speed Press
P.O. Box 7123
Berkeley, California 94707

Cover and book design
by Michael Mabry.

Photography by
Noreen Rei Fukumori.

Distributed in Australia
by Simon & Schuster
Australia; in Canada
by Publishers Group West;
in New Zealand by Tandem
Press; in South Africa by
Real Books; in Singapore,
Malasia, and Indonesia by
Berkeley Books; and in the
United Kingdom by Airlift Books.

Library of Congress Cataloging-in-Publication Data

Pawlcyn, Cindy
   The Fog City Diner cookbook/by Cindy Pawlcyn.

   Includes bibliographical references.
      1. Cookery   2. Fog City Diner.   I. Title.

TX714.P385   1992   641.5'09794'61–dc20   92-42160

ISBN 0-890815-493-6

Printed in Hong Kong

4 5 6 7 8 9 10 — 02 01 00 99 98

DEDICATION

This book is dedicated to Stephen Pawlcyn, Sr., and Murdo Laird

I wish to thank the following people for their support, help, patience, and encouragement: Robert Cubberly, Jennifer Palmer, Vicky Pardus, Charles Tobey, Joe Peck, Dorothy Pawlcyn, Lois Lee, Yvonne and Ned Moody, Barbara Neyers, Jackie Wan, and George Young. Special thanks to John Harrisson who assisted in the early stages of formulating and planning this project; to Julie Hall and the people she had testing recipes; to Joanna Axelrod and Peter Franck; to Michael Mabry for design and Noreen Rei Fukumori for photographs; to Terry Lynch and the gang at Mustards; to Gordon Drysdale and the gang at Bix; to Manny Goodman and the gang at Roti; to Michael Chiarello and the gang at Tra Vigne; to Bob Martin and the gang at Buckeye Roadhouse; and of course, to everyone at the Fog City Diner, including all those wonderful customers who keep us there. Above all, thanks to my two partners, Bill Higgins and Bill Upson.

GET IN HERE!

Table of Contents

Let's face it, we got in this crazy business because we like to have fun. That's why Cindy,

Bill [Upson], and I opened Mustards Grill in Napa Valley--after working our tails off for

other fine restaurateurs, we wanted to be the ones to put together the good food and

good times. We had no money, so we built it and ran it ourselves. Furiously, we blended

cement, stain, linoleum, and paint, and threw in a little chardonnay to keep us going.

Cindy cooked nonstop. Bill did the grill and the books. I waited tables and

answered the phone. It was fun, and we were hooked. After that, Fog City

Diner had to happen. We were on a mission and San Francisco was our target. I remember

driving back to the Bay Area so many times from Mustards--planning, scheming,

knowing it all had to come true. We just had to put all the ingredients together--you

know--like a recipe.... 3 Tons of Energy There is a kinetic energy that charges the

Fog City Diner, like how Cindy, Bill, and I can't sit still for one minute [combined]. I wish you could have seen the place being constructed. It was like an ant colony swarming on absinthe. The Diner was designed on cocktail napkins. Many of the contractors were  "fly-[or something]-by-night," so we never knew what, if anything, was going to get done on time. The date of the opening party [June 16, 1985] had been set for months, but the night before the party, the Diner still had no floor. So there we were, on hands and knees, setting tile until four in the morning so the big shots we had invited to the party would have a place to stand. I remember a well-known San Francisco designer asking me, "How'd you get the floor to look so beat up and screwy, like it's been here for years?"

60 Years of Diner History   Everybody loves a diner. Why? It's comfortable, and it's affordable. It's unintimidating. It's accommodating. It's American. It's colorful. It's shiny. And it's fun. So we just added a new chapter to this history -- everything you could want from a diner plus what's happening today. The sign on the front door says "No Crybabies." This means anything goes --have a good time, and leave your problems elsewhere.   2 Different Menus in One

The menu is balanced so there is something for everybody. Half of the menu is what you'd expect--hamburgers, fries, and malts, etc., but updated and thought out, using only

fresh,  quality ingredients. [What other diner uses top sirloin in its chili?]

The other half is the new stuff; innovative and unusual dishes with small

enough portions so you can enjoy all kinds of different tastes in one meal. We

call it "dim sum and then some." **A Moderate Amount of Anything You Can**

Imagine to Drink Sure, sure there are sodas, milk shakes, and egg

creams. But hey, San Franciscans need more than that! With the help of

friends in Napa Valley we put together a great wine list with every varietal

represented. Want a beer? We've got over a dozen. What's better than an ice-cold Anchor

Steam and a dozen Kumomoto oysters when you've got the need?

[We've heard the Diner called "the ultimate hangover

restaurant."] The well-lit back bar boasts one of the largest

selections of single malt Scotches in The City. Cocktails? Every one you've ever heard of,

including some that date back to prehistoric times. **20 Cooks 2 Bakers 18 Waiters**

7 Bartenders 4 Hosts 6 Dishwashers 8 Bussers Even before we opened, all these

people got into the act. They knew where the Diner was going, and they

were determined to play a part. They do their jobs professionally, but with a great sense of humor. Much of the spirit of the Diner comes from this great staff. Just ask 'em. **1 City That Knows How** There's something about San Francisco that makes you want to go out and have fun, whether you're in tuxedos or tennis clothes. I think it's in the city code or something. It's a restaurant-crazy town, and we fit right in. **800,000 Customers** Whether they are native San Franciscans, transplants, or tourists, our customers are here to take part in that grand San Francisco tradition called dining out. And whether they get  here in a limousine, on a ten-speed bike, or on foot, our aim is to make sure that they have a good time here--even if it means serving up a 40th wedding anniversary dinner of Diner Chili Dogs with Roederer Cristal Champagne to wash it down. **1 Great Chef** Cindy is really the one who made it all happen, and she's still cooking it up here as she has from day one. I never thought Cindy would do it, though. All these recipes that made Fog City Diner famous made public? But what the heck. You're not going to open a diner, right? So why not share all this good food [and a cocktail or two] with those of you who couldn't get a reservation tonight. Bill Higgins February 1993 P.S. We'll still be open tomorrow, so "Get In Here!"

Well, Boo's intro seems to sum it all up pretty well. [I call Bill Higgins "Boo" and Bill Upson "Up" to keep from getting my two partners mixed up.] The three of us had always wanted a diner that suited our eating tastes, not a 24-hour breakfast-and-greasy spoon kinda diner, but one you felt comfortable in whether you wanted a pre-opera meal or a post-game snack, a home away from home where food was made from scratch with the best ingredients available and served up at reasonable prices. I think we've succeeded well. We've gone on to open a number of other restaurants [Roti and Bix in The City; Buckeye Roadhouse in Mill Valley; and Tra Vigne in Napa Valley], and Mustards is still going strong. Of them all, though, I'd have to say that nothing can beat the Diner for just plain fun. This book follows the format of the Diner's menu. It includes most of our Diner standards, plus recipes for dishes that are special favorites of our customers, friends, family, and staff. Please feel free to experiment with these recipes, as nothing is carved in stone. I hope that they bring enjoyment to your home dining.

CINDY PAWLCYN FEBRUARY 1993

This is the last restaurant I am laying the tile in!

BILL UPSON FEBRUARY 1993

BRE

CHAP

ADS

TER 1

BREADS
CHAPTER 1

When we first opened up Fog City Diner, our plan was to have everything made in-house, including all the breads and rolls. We've stuck by this pretty well, even though making bread in a restaurant is very labor-intensive. The only breads we buy are the Italian-style loaves, which we use for the Leek and Basil Loaf, and our burger buns (we just go through too many to make them ourselves). The hot dog buns, po' boy rolls, and tortillas, as well as all the specialty breads, are still made in-house.   When I was growing up, my mom baked white bread at home, big huge batches of it. I loved to eat the heel of a loaf hot from the oven, loaded with butter, and sprinkled with sugar. I still think there is nothing better than the smell of bread baking. Not a whole lot of things anyway. I would regularly help my mom knead the dough, and in no time, I was baking bread by myself.   Making bread is a piece of cake. Flour, water, yeast, and some practice is all there is to it. So don't be intimidated—make bread as often as you can and you'll soon develop a feel for it.   In most of the recipes that follow, yeast is used for leavening. Yeast should be dissolved in a lukewarm liquid (105 to 115 degrees) to activate it. Most yeast doughs must be kneaded, either by hand or in a mixer. As a rule of thumb, you should knead the dough for 3 to 5 minutes or until it becomes smooth and satiny, then let it rise until it doubles in volume. The dough should then be punched down, shaped, and allowed to rise a second time. Occasionally we use the sponge method, which requires three risings (the Cheddar Cheese Buns are made this way). Most bread doughs can also be made into rolls or buns. If you want, you could make half of the dough into rolls and form the rest into a loaf, or make nothing but rolls. There are a variety of flours available. At home I use all-purpose unbleached white flour, which is a blend of hard and soft wheats. (I tested all the recipes at home using all-purpose unbleached flour, and they all turned out fine.) Our bakers at the Diner use bread flour, which is made from hard wheat and is higher in gluten and has more protein. Either of these flours will work well for all the breads and rolls. Cake flour is made from soft wheat. A portion of cake flour in the biscuit recipe will result in a lighter, flakier biscuit. The flour amounts in the recipes are somewhat flexible. You may need to add a bit more or a bit less than is called for. The important thing is to develop a smooth, satiny feel to the dough during the kneading process. Of course freshness of ingredients is very important to the success of these recipes. Be careful to store flour in a dry, cool place, and keep it away from other food with strong odors. Feel free to change the recipes if you want to. For example, you could substitute a portion of the white flour with another flour or grain. You can also experiment with baking techniques. Try baking the bread free-form on clay baking tiles. If you like a crusty bread, preheat a small pan in the oven and fill it with ice just before putting the bread in. The steam will provide the necessary humidity for a crisper crust. Slashing the top of the shaped dough with a sharp knife or a razor blade just before putting it into the oven will allow the bread to expand rapidly without cracking. Cool the bread on a rack to keep the bottom of the loaf from becoming soggy. Bread will slice better if it is cooled first—but nothing beats warm bread and butter. The best thing about baking bread is that you learn how to trust your own taste and judgment. Don't be afraid. Go ahead and experiment. The recipes will still work.

Diner White Bread

This is a rich basic bread that reminds me of the bread
my mom used to make. It's great for toast or grilled cheese sandwiches.
The dough can also be made into rolls or buns. You can
substitute a little whole wheat flour or other grains and cereals to vary
the texture and flavor.

MAKES 4 LOAVES OR 12 TO 16 ROLLS

2	packages active dry yeast
2	cups lukewarm water
2	cups milk
¼	cup unsalted butter, at room temperature
3	tablespoons sugar
9-10	cups flour
1½	teaspoons kosher or sea salt
1	tablespoon olive oil Dutch Crunch Topping (recipe follows) or 2 tablespoons softened butter

In a large bowl, sprinkle the yeast over 1 cup of the lukewarm water, stir, and let sit for 10 minutes to dissolve the yeast. Meanwhile combine the milk, remaining 1 cup water, butter, and sugar in a saucepan and heat until the butter is melted. Cool to lukewarm, and stir into the yeast mixture.

Gradually add the flour and salt, mixing with a wooden spoon until the dough is thoroughly combined. Transfer the dough to a lightly floured smooth surface and knead for about 3 to 5 minutes until satiny and slightly resilient to the touch. If the dough is sticky, add a little flour as you knead it.

Lightly brush a bowl with half the oil. Add the dough and rotate it until coated with oil. Cover the bowl with a damp towel or plastic wrap, and let the dough rise in a warm place until it doubles in volume, about 1 hour. Punch the dough down and knead briefly.

Lightly brush four 9 x 5-inch loaf pans with the remaining oil. Divide the dough into 4 equal pieces and roll them into loaves, making sure all air bubbles are patted out. Place the loaves in the pans. If you're making rolls, shape the dough into rolls and place them on a baking

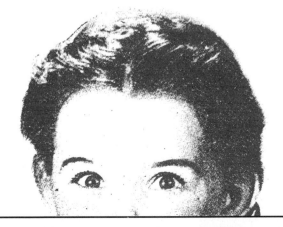

sheet lined with parchment. For a crustier roll, sprinkle some cornmeal on the parchment first, or just use an ungreased pan sprinkled with cornmeal.

If you are using Dutch Crunch, spread the topping over the loaves or rolls at this point. Cover loosely with a damp towel or plastic wrap and let rise in a warm place for about 1 hour or until the loaves or rolls have doubled in size.

Preheat the oven to 350 degrees about 30 minutes before baking. Bake the loaves for 50 minutes to 1 hour, or until the crust is golden brown and the bottom of the loaves sound hollow when tapped lightly. Rolls should bake for 25 to 40 minutes. Remove from the oven, and if you did not use the Dutch Crunch option, brush the crust while hot with the 2 tablespoons of softened butter. Turn onto a rack to cool.

Dutch Crunch Topping

The Dutch Crunch Topping makes for a more crusty top, and adds a little sweetness to the bread. The topping should be spread on the bread with a spoon prior to the last rise. The following ingredients will make enough topping for four loaves.

1	tablespoon sugar
1	ounce (4 packages) active dry yeast
¾	cup rice flour
1	teaspoon salt
1	tablespoon olive oil
½	cup water

Combine the sugar, yeast, rice flour, and salt in a small bowl. With a wooden spoon mix in the olive oil and water. The topping should be the consistency of yogurt. Add more water if it seems too thick. Let the mixture stand for 15 minutes. Spread on the bread or rolls after they have been shaped but before the final rising.

Cheddar Cheese Buns

These buns are a favorite among the staff at the Diner, especially with Joe Peck,
our general manager. They are great accompaniments for chili and soups;
on their own they're like a cheese sandwich (mini ones are great for parties).
As long as the cheddar cheese stands out as the main flavor, you can use up odd
bits of other kinds of cheese for these buns. For a different flavor, you can
substitute a cup of bleu cheese for the asiago or Jarlsberg cheese and add a cup of
toasted chopped walnuts to the filling. It's best to refrigerate the
dough overnight for a slow second rise. These buns should be served warm.

MAKES 16 TO 18 BUNS

1	package active dry yeast
¼	cup lukewarm water
5½	cups flour
4	tablespoons sugar
2	teaspoons kosher or sea salt
1¼	cups butter, cut into pieces
6	eggs

Cheese Filling:

5-6	cloves garlic
2	cups grated cheddar cheese
1	cup grated asiago or Jarlsberg cheese (or a combination, or more cheddar)
2	tablespoons minced chives or scallions
2	tablespoons minced Italian parsley
2	tablespoons minced basil leaves
1	teaspoon freshly ground white pepper
1	egg beaten with ½ cup milk (for egg wash)

In a medium-sized bowl, sprinkle the yeast over the lukewarm water, stir, and let sit for 10 minutes to dissolve the yeast. Place the flour, sugar, and salt in the bowl of a mixer. Add the butter, and with a paddle attachment, combine until the mixture resembles coarse cornmeal.

Beat the eggs in another bowl, then combine them with the yeast. Add this liquid mixture to the dry ingredients in the mixer. Change to a dough hook and mix thoroughly, stopping occasionally to push the dough down from the hook. The dough will be very soft. Mix 3 minutes on medium-high speed. Shape it into a ball, cover with a damp towel or plastic wrap, and let the dough rise in a warm place for 3 hours. Punch the dough down again, and refrigerate overnight to rise again.

To make the cheese filling, put the garlic in a pan with cold water to cover. Bring to a rolling boil and drain. Repeat two more times, then mince the blanched garlic. Mix together with the other filling ingredients. Reserve.

Transfer the dough to a smooth floured surface and roll it out in a jelly roll-sized rectangle to a ⅔-inch thickness. Sprinkle the filling evenly on top of the dough. Roll up the dough like a jelly roll, and cut it into 16 to 18 slices about 1½ inches thick. For each bun, pinch the edges of one cut side together to keep the filling from oozing out, and place, pinched side down, on a parchment-lined baking sheet. I have also baked these in flattened paper muffin cups and in nonstick baking pans. Cover loosely with a damp towel or plastic wrap and let rise in a warm place for about 1½ hours.

Preheat the oven to 375 degrees. Brush the buns with the egg wash and bake for 20 minutes, or until golden brown and the cheese begins to melt. Slide the buns onto a rack to cool. They are best served warm.

Hamburger Buns

The true test of a good hamburger bun is that you can take a bite out of one side of it without the burger slipping out the other side. This dough is untraditional in that you start out by cutting the butter into the dry ingredients as you would for a pie dough. This is what makes the buns very tender and allows them to pass the true test described above.

Although we don't make our own hamburger buns anymore, we still use this dough to make hot dog buns and po' boys. Instructions for shaping all will follow.

MAKES 16 BUNS OR ROLLS

2   packages active dry yeast
2   cups lukewarm water
6-7   cups unbleached flour
     (or 5 cups unbleached white flour plus 1-2 cups whole wheat flour)
2   teaspoons kosher or sea salt
2   tablespoons sugar
4   tablespoons unsalted butter, cut into pieces
½   cup olive oil plus extra to coat the bowl
2   tablespoons cornmeal
1   egg beaten with ½ cup milk (for egg wash)
3   tablespoons seeds (sesame, poppy, caraway, cumin, fennel, etc.)

In a medium bowl, sprinkle the yeast over the lukewarm water, stir, and let sit for 10 minutes to dissolve the yeast. Combine the flour, salt, and sugar in a large bowl and cut in the softened butter until the mixture resembles coarse crumbs. Add the yeast mixture and olive oil, and continue mixing until all the ingredients come together. Transfer the dough to a smooth floured surface and knead for 3 to 5 minutes or until the dough is satiny and elastic. If the dough is very sticky, you might need to work in an additional ¼ cup flour. This is a very tender and soft dough.

Lightly brush a bowl with olive oil. Add the dough and rotate it to coat it with the oil. Cover the bowl with a damp towel or plastic wrap, and let the dough rise in a warm place until it doubles in volume, about 1 hour. Punch the dough down and knead briefly. Line a baking sheet with parchment paper and sprinkle it with 1 to 2 tablespoons cornmeal.

Divide the dough into equal pieces (3½ ounces each), form into balls, and roll out to 3- to 4-inch diameter circles. Place the buns on the baking sheet, cover with a damp towel or plastic wrap, and let rise in a warm place for 30 minutes. Press each bun down slightly to compress it. Brush the buns with the egg wash, sprinkle liberally with seeds, and let rise again in a warm place for 30 to 45 minutes, until rolls have doubled in size.

To form Hot Dog Buns, divide the dough into equal pieces (2½ ounces each), press flat, and roll into cigar shapes about 4½ inches long. Place seam-side down on the prepared baking sheet. Brush with egg wash, and sprinkle liberally with the seeds of your choice (caraway seeds are good with Polish sausage or bratwurst, cumin seeds with chorizo, and fennel seeds with Italian sausage might be nice). Let rolls rise in a warm place for 1 hour until they have doubled in size.

For Po' Boys, roll out all the dough into one large rectangle about ¼ inch thick. Cut into 3 x 5-inch rectangles. Place the rolls on the prepared baking sheet, brush with egg wash, and sprinkle with seeds—poppy seeds are my favorite. Let rise until doubled in size, about 1 hour.

Preheat the oven to 375 degrees. Bake for about 20 to 30 minutes, or until golden brown. Turn onto a rack to cool. Let cool completely before using.

Potato Poppy Seed Rolls

These simple, classic, flavorful rolls are the perfect thing for
sopping up sauces. To make them, you need to boil a couple of potatoes first.
Save the potato water: that goes into the dough, too.
You could use warmed leftover mashed potatoes and plain water,
though the result would not be quite as good.

MAKES ABOUT 24 LARGE ROLLS

2	packages active dry yeast
¼	cup lukewarm water
1	cup warm mashed potatoes
1½	cups lukewarm potato water
½	cup unsalted butter, cut into ½-inch pieces
1½	teaspoons kosher or sea salt
¼	cup sugar
6-7	cups flour
2	teaspoons olive oil or softened butter
1	tablespoon cornmeal
1	egg beaten with ½ cup milk (for egg wash)
½	cup poppy seeds

In a small bowl, sprinkle the yeast over the lukewarm water, stir, and let sit for 10 minutes to dissolve the yeast. In a large bowl, using a wooden spoon, combine the potatoes, potato water, butter, salt, and sugar, and stir until the ingredients are well mixed. The warm potatoes should melt the butter. Add the yeast mixture to the potatoes, then slowly incorporate 6 to 7 cups of flour in 1 cup increments. Mix for 5 minutes. Transfer the dough to a lightly floured smooth surface and knead for about 10 minutes until satiny but slightly soft, so the rolls remain tender.

Lightly brush a bowl with the oil. Add the dough and rotate it until thoroughly coated with the oil. Cover the bowl with a damp towel or plastic wrap, and let the dough rise in a warm place until it doubles in volume, about 1 to 1½ hours. Punch the dough down and let it rest for 10 to 15 minutes.

Line a baking sheet with parchment paper and sprinkle it with the cornmeal. Cut the dough into 24 or so pieces and form the rolls by rolling each piece in a circular motion on a smooth surface, or roll them into ropes and tie the ropes in a knot. Brush the rolls with the egg wash and sprinkle them with poppy seeds. (Poppy seed lovers may want to dip the ropes of dough in egg wash and roll them in poppy seeds to thoroughly coat them before tying the knots.)

Cover the rolls loosely with plastic wrap and let them rise in a warm place for 45 minutes to 1 hour, until they have almost doubled in size. Preheat oven to 350 degrees. Bake rolls for 20 to 25 minutes or until golden brown.

Caraway Rye Bread

This light-textured rye bread is great sliced and griddled,
especially for corned beef or Reuben sandwiches.
The recipe can also be made into Kaiser-style rolls, or if you're feeling
inspired, divide the dough into 6 equal pieces,
roll them out into ropes, and braid them into 2 loaves.

MAKES 2 LOAVES

2	packages active dry yeast
¼	cup brown sugar, firmly packed
1	cup lukewarm water
1	cup milk
½	cup unsalted butter, cut into pieces
4¼	cups all-purpose flour
1	cup rye flour
2	teaspoons kosher or sea salt
¼	cup caraway seeds
2	teaspoons olive oil
2	tablespoons cornmeal
	Milk for brushing top of loaves

In a large bowl sprinkle the yeast and sugar over the water, stir, and let sit for 10 minutes to dissolve. Place the milk and butter in a saucepan and heat to melt the butter. Cool to lukewarm, and stir into the yeast mixture.

In another mixing bowl, combine 1¼ cups flour, the rye flour, salt, and half the caraway seeds. Add this to the yeast mixture in ½ cup increments, mixing for 2 minutes after each addition. Continue mixing while adding the remaining 3 cups flour in ½ cup increments. As the dough becomes difficult to mix, turn it onto a lightly floured smooth surface and knead for 5 or 6 minutes, until all the ingredients are thoroughly incorporated.

Lightly brush a bowl with the oil. Add the dough and rotate it to coat it with oil. Cover the bowl with a damp towel or plastic wrap, and let the dough rise in a warm place until it doubles in volume, about 1 hour. Punch the dough down and knead vigorously, about 1 minute. Let the dough rest for a few minutes. It will become less elastic and be easier to form into loaves.

Line a baking sheet with parchment paper and sprinkle it with the cornmeal. Shape the dough into 2 large free-form loaves (or make 2 braided loaves) and set them on the baking sheet. Brush the loaves with a little milk and sprinkle them with the remaining caraway seeds. Cover loosely with a damp towel or plastic wrap and let rise in a warm place for about 1 hour.

Preheat the oven to 350 degrees about 30 minutes before baking. Bake for 50 minutes to 1 hour, or until the crust is well browned and the bottom of the loaves sound hollow when tapped lightly. Remove from oven and turn onto a rack to cool. Reduce the baking time for rolls.

Steam Beer Bread

We use Anchor Steam Beer to make this bread; it's a local beer,
produced here in San Francisco. If you have a local brewery,
you may want to try their beer. Just be sure to use a good-tasting beer
because it will make a difference in how the bread tastes.
This bread is really good for ham-and-cheese sandwiches or with roast pork.
Like the Cheddar Cheese Buns, it is made by the sponge method,
which involves three rises. The recipe also makes great rolls:
just shorten the baking time a little.

MAKES 2 LOAVES

2   packages active dry yeast
4   tablespoons granulated or brown sugar
½   cup lukewarm milk
1   cup (¾ bottle) beer, at room temperature
6   cups flour
1   tablespoon kosher or sea salt
½   cup unsalted butter, cut into small pieces
4   eggs
2   teaspoons olive oil

In a large mixing bowl, sprinkle the yeast and sugar over the milk, stir, and let sit for 10 minutes to dissolve. Add the beer and 2 cups of the flour and mix thoroughly to form a sponge. Cover the bowl with a damp towel or plastic wrap, and let the sponge rise in a warm place until it doubles in volume, about 1 hour.

Put 3 cups of flour and the salt and butter in the bowl of a mixer, and using the paddle attachment, cut the butter in as you would for a pie dough. Change to a dough hook, add the sponge and eggs, and mix thoroughly, stopping occasionally to remove dough from the hook. Knead in as much of the remaining flour as necessary to keep the dough satiny. Transfer the dough to a lightly floured smooth surface and knead for 5 to 10 minutes, until satiny and slightly resilient to the touch.

Lightly brush a bowl with 1 teaspoon of oil. Add the dough and rotate it to coat it with oil. Cover the bowl with a damp towel or plastic wrap, and let the dough rise in a warm place until it doubles in volume, about 1 hour. Punch the dough down.

Lightly brush two 9 x 5-inch loaf pans with the remaining oil. Roll the dough into loaves and place them in the pans. Cover loosely with a damp towel or plastic wrap, and let rise in a warm place for about 45 minutes to 1 hour, until the loaves have doubled in size.

Preheat the oven to 375 degrees about 30 minutes before baking. Bake the loaves for 40 to 45 minutes, or until the crust is golden brown and the bottom of the loaves sound hollow when tapped lightly.

Jalapeño Corn Stix

This recipe started out as corn muffins, but I've found that baking the
dough in corn stick molds gives the bread a great crispy texture.
You can buy cast-iron molds in hardware stores, but you have to season
them before you use them for the first time. Oil the molds and
put them in a 400-degree oven for 1 hour.
These corn sticks go well with chili, hot dogs, soups, chicken, fried fish,
and anything barbecued. For a milder corn stick, substitute
red bell pepper for the jalapeño.

MAKES ABOUT 16 CORN STICKS OR 12 MEDIUM-SIZED MUFFINS

Dry Ingredients:

¾ cup yellow or white cornmeal
1½ cups flour
¼ cup sugar
1½ teaspoons baking powder
½ teaspoon baking soda
½ teaspoon kosher or sea salt
1 cup grated Tillamook cheese, or
   sharp or medium cheddar cheese
2 teaspoons finely diced, roasted,
   and seeded jalapeño chiles
   (or 2 mounded tablespoons diced
   and seeded red bell pepper)
1 scallion, finely minced
½ cup fresh corn kernels (1 medium
   ear of corn)
3 tablespoons chopped cilantro

Liquid Ingredients:

1 cup buttermilk
4 tablespoons unsalted butter,
   melted
2 eggs
1 tablespoon peanut oil

Preheat the oven to 400 degrees,
and heat the corn stick molds. In a
large bowl, mix together all the dry
ingredients including the cheese,
jalapeños, scallion, corn, and cilantro. In a separate bowl, whisk together the buttermilk, butter, and
eggs, and then slowly stir in the dry
ingredients with a wooden spoon,
just until moistened.

Remove the hot molds from the
oven and lightly brush them with
the peanut oil. Fill the molds three-
fourths full using a ladle, wooden
spoon, or a pastry bag without
a nozzle. Bake 20 to 25 minutes or
until the edges are golden and a
toothpick comes out clean.

To make muffins, grease muffin
tins or line them with paper cups.
Fill them three-fourths full and
bake as for corn sticks.

Buttery Leek and Basil Loaf

I stole the idea for this recipe from my mom—from the way she made
garlic bread, anyway. This is one bread that we
don't bake from scratch. We use loaves of Italian bread that
we get from a local baker, and add a generous amount of
herbed butter. If you don't have a specialty bread available, use
a crusty white or sourdough loaf.
Any leftover butter is good on grilled chicken or fish.

MAKES 1 LARGE ITALIAN LOAF OR 2 FRENCH BAGUETTES

2   tablespoons minced parsley leaves

1   cup unsalted butter, at room temperature

¾-1   cup thinly sliced leeks, washed and blanched

½   tablespoon minced thyme leaves

1½   tablespoons minced chives or scallions

2   tablespoons minced tarragon leaves

2   tablespoons minced basil leaves

½   tablespoon minced chervil (or extra basil or parsley)

½   teaspoon kosher or sea salt
Freshly ground white pepper to taste

1   large crusty Italian loaf, or 2 crusty French baguettes

Rinse the parsley; place it in a towel and twist to squeeze out any moisture. This removes the excess chlorophyll, making the parsley less grassy tasting. Combine the butter, leeks, herbs, salt, and pepper together using a mixer, or by hand with a wooden spoon.

Preheat the oven to 375 degrees. Cut slices in the bread 1 inch apart and about three-fourths of the way through the loaf, so that the slices are still attached at the base of the loaf. There should be at least 12 slices. Spread a generous table-spoon of the herb butter in each slice, and spread any remaining butter over the top of the bread. Bake the bread for 15 to 20 minutes, until the butter has melted and the bread is crusty. You may also heat this bread by wrapping in alumi-num foil and grilling it over a wood or charcoal fire. Be sure to turn it often for even heating.

Flour Tortillas

Homemade tortillas are so much better than store-bought, and they're so simple to make that once you try it and taste the difference, you may never buy tortillas again. The size is up to you—you can make them large or small, or even cut them into odd shapes. Tortillas are useful items to have around for whipping up quesadillas (page 62), or for serving with chilis and stews. They are even good just warmed up and spread with butter. Leftover tortillas freeze well: just allow them to cool first and wrap them in foil.

MAKES ABOUT TWENTY 10-INCH TORTILLAS

4 cups flour
2 teaspoons kosher or sea salt
1 teaspoon baking powder
1 cup unsalted butter, cut in thin slices
1 cup cold water

Combine the flour, salt, and baking powder in a large bowl. Cut in the butter until the mixture resembles coarse crumbs. Add the water and continue mixing just until the ingredients are incorporated. Do not overmix.

Shape the dough into a log about 3½ inches in diameter. Cover with plastic wrap and chill for about 1 hour. Uncover, and cut the dough evenly into about 20 slices. On a lightly floured smooth surface, roll out the slices, and using a plate as a guide, cut them into 10-inch circles, or whatever size you prefer.

Stack the tortillas with waxed paper in between. Refrigerate and allow to rest for about 30 minutes. Cook the tortillas on a hot ungreased griddle or in a cast-iron pan, turning frequently until they are cooked through and the dough is no longer translucent. At this point, the tortillas can be filled for quesadillas and finished later or just stacked as they are and reserved in the refrigerator for later use. If you plan on serving them immediately, continue cooking until golden brown specks appear on the surface of each side. To reheat tortillas, stick them in a warm oven for a few minutes, or heat them quickly on a griddle or in a cast-iron pan with no oil added.

Buttermilk Biscuits

We make these biscuits especially for our "Chicken on a Bisquit" plate (page 136). They also go well with soups and stews, and with scrambled eggs for breakfast. To keep the biscuits tender, work quickly and avoid overmixing. The dough tends to be very moist, so it's a good idea to keep your fingers and the work surface well dusted with flour. For a savory variation, add 3 minced scallions to the dry ingredients before mixing. Substituting part cake flour will result in a lighter biscuit.

MAKES 12 BISCUITS

2½   cups all-purpose flour or 2 cups all-purpose flour and ½ cup cake flour
1¼   tablespoons baking powder
1   teaspoon kosher or sea salt
2   tablespoons sugar
7   tablespoons unsalted butter
1   large egg
¾   cup buttermilk
1   egg beaten with ½ cup milk (for optional egg wash)

Combine the flour, baking powder, salt, and sugar in a large bowl. Cut in the butter until the mixture is the consistency of coarse meal. In a separate bowl, mix together 1 egg and the buttermilk, and add this all at once to the flour and butter mixture. Working quickly, mix just until all the ingredients are moist and the dough comes together. Do not overmix.

Preheat the oven to 375 degrees. Transfer the dough to a smooth, well-floured surface. Roll or pat the dough to a ¾-inch thickness and cut with a 3-inch cookie or biscuit cutter. You can also cut the dough into squares. Place on a baking sheet lined with parchment paper so the biscuits are touching each other. If you want to glaze the biscuits, brush them with the egg wash or with a little buttermilk (buttermilk will give the same effect).

Bake the biscuits for about 20 minutes or until golden. Slide them onto a rack to cool.

BO

CHAP

BOWLS

CHAPTER 2

I think of soup as the ultimate comfort food, a feeling that probably goes back to my younger days in Minnesota. Once, when I was a teenager, I made up what I thought of as the perfect batch of chicken soup. I was so excited I called my grandmother to invite her over to try it. "Sure," she said. "I'd love to. Who is this?" "You mean you'd go out for lunch without knowing who invited you?" I asked. "Sure," she said. "You think I'm crazy? I love soup." I like to think she would have loved any of the soups we serve at the Diner.   On our menu, all soups come under the heading of "bowls," along with any other dishes that are too soupy to be eaten with a fork. This includes chowders, stews, and our Sirloin and Black Bean Chili (which my husband does eat with a fork).   When you prepare soups, be sure all the ingredients are cut small enough so that they can be easily picked up in a spoon. Your guests won't enjoy their meal if they can't get their mouths around it. Serve the more substantial bowls in sturdy, broad-based bowls so that there is room to maneuver around the shells or bones. Also, remember to provide extra plates for bones and shells, and warm damp napkins and lemon wedges for sticky fingers.

Roasted Sweet Red Pepper and Potato Soup

To make the soup more colorful, use a combination of red, yellow, and orange bell peppers. And if you want to dress it up a little more, you can garnish it with pesto, croutons, or minced fresh herbs. For a chowderlike consistency, do not purée the soup, but be sure to cut the peppers, onion, and potatoes into neat uniform dice.

4-5	large red bell peppers
1	large or 2 medium yellow onions, diced
1-2	cloves garlic, minced
3	tablespoons olive oil
6	cups Chicken Stock (page 223) or Vegetable Stock (page 224)
2	medium potatoes, peeled and diced
¼-½	cup heavy cream (optional)
3	tablespoons chopped basil
	Kosher or sea salt
	Freshly ground pepper

Roast, peel, seed, and dice the bell peppers. Heat the oil in a large pot, and sauté the onion and garlic over medium heat until translucent. Add the bell peppers and stock, and cook for 10 minutes. Add the potatoes and cook until tender.

Purée the soup, if desired, and strain it into a clean pot. Add the cream, basil, salt, and pepper. Stir and bring just to a boil. (Note: If you are using light cream, heat the soup gently and take extra care not to boil it.)

Ginger and Carrot Soup

The flavors of ginger and carrot combine together really well. The clean, light taste of this soup makes it a great way to start a meal. It's good hot or cold, with or without the cream.

2	tablespoons unsalted butter or olive oil
1	medium white onion, cut into large dice
3	large carrots, peeled and sliced
1½	stalks celery, chopped
2	large cloves garlic, chopped
1	1-inch piece of ginger, peeled and finely grated
4	cups Chicken Stock (page 223)
½	cup heavy cream (optional)
5-6	sprigs cilantro, chopped
	Kosher or sea salt
	Freshly ground pepper to taste
2	tablespoons minced scallions
3	tablespoons sour cream or yogurt (optional)

In a large pot, melt the butter over medium heat. Add the onion, carrots, celery, garlic, and ginger, and cook until tender, stirring occasionally. When the vegetables begin to caramelize, add the stock and simmer until the carrots are tender, about 45 minutes. Purée and strain the soup into a clean pot. Add the optional cream, cilantro, salt, and pepper; stir and bring to a simmer. If you are serving the soup cold, chill it, then check the seasonings before serving it. It might need more salt and pepper. Serve garnished with scallions and optional sour cream or yogurt.

Corn and Pasilla Chile Chowder

My favorite way to eat corn is to boil a pot of water, run out
to the garden for a few ears of fresh corn, cook the corn immediately,
rub it with butter, add a sprinkle of salt, and eat it off the cob.
Of course that scenario has its limits. This chowder is my second
favorite way to eat corn. Fortunately, it has no limits.

SERVES 6

3	fresh pasilla chiles (or poblano or Anaheim chiles)
3	ears of corn, shucked and kernels cut off the cob (2½ cups)
5	cups Chicken Stock (page 223)
2	tablespoons olive oil or butter
1½	cups diced onion
¾	cup chopped celery
½	cup chopped parsnips
2	medium-sized russet potatoes, peeled and diced
1-1½	cups cream
	Kosher or sea salt
	Freshly ground pepper
	Chopped chives, for garnish

Roast, peel, and seed the chiles, and cut them into small dice. Put the corn cobs in the chicken stock and bring to a boil. Simmer 20 to 30 minutes until there is a pronounced corn flavor to the stock. Remove the cobs.

Heat the olive oil or butter in a saucepan; add the onion and celery, and cook covered over very low heat for 2 to 3 minutes. Add the pasillas, parsnips, potatoes, and stock. Simmer until the potatoes and parsnips are cooked through, about 15 to 20 minutes. Add the cream, corn kernels, salt, and pepper; stir and simmer another 2 minutes. Adjust seasoning, if necessary. Serve garnished with chopped chives.

Leek and Pear Soup

This soup is delicious served either cold or hot, but you may want to
increase some of the seasonings if you serve it cold.
Taste it and adjust the seasonings before serving. Because of the sweetness
of the pears, either tarragon or chervil will work nicely, but
for a spicier flavor, you could use summer savory instead. You can substitute
apples or carrots for the pears, and sweet or white onions
or scallions for the leeks.

SERVES 4 TO 6

3	tablespoons unsalted butter
1	large leek, washed and chopped
3	pears, peeled, cored, and quartered
½	cup white wine
3	cups Chicken Stock (page 223) or Vegetable Stock (page 224)
2	teaspoons minced tarragon or sprigs of chervil
½	cup heavy cream (optional)
	Kosher or sea salt
	Freshly ground pepper

Garnish:

½	cup Crème Fraîche (page 169) or lightly whipped cream
	Finely minced tarragon or additional sprigs of chervil

Melt the butter in a large pot, and simmer the leek, covered, over medium-low heat for about 10 to 15 minutes, until tender but not browned. Add the pears and wine and bring to a boil. Add the stock and simmer until the pears are cooked through. Purée the soup. Strain it, if desired, and put it into a clean pot. Add the tarragon or chervil and optional cream, and season to taste. Return to a simmer.

Divide the soup evenly between bowls and garnish each serving with a dollop of crème fraîche or lightly whipped cream, and a sprinkle of the herbs.

French Onion Soup

I suppose it's not surprising that the first really good onion soup I
ever tasted was in Paris. The secret, I have since learned,
is to use very good stocks. Be sure to cut the onions from top to bottom
rather than in rings; they are more tender that way and are
easier to eat. Above all, resist the temptation to use too much cheese.

SERVES 6

4 ounces fontina cheese

4 ounces Jarlsberg cheese

4 ounces asiago or parmesan cheese

3 tablespoons unsalted butter

2 tablespoons olive oil

3½ pounds yellow onions, thinly sliced from top to bottom

10 cloves garlic, minced

10 shallots, minced

1 bay leaf

½ tablespoon kosher or sea salt

1½ teaspoons freshly ground white pepper

2 tablespoons brandy

4 tablespoons Madeira

1 cup white wine

3 cups Veal Stock or Beef Stock (page 222)

3 cups Chicken Stock (page 223)

1 crouton per serving (page 228)

Grate all the cheeses, mix well, and reserve.

Heat the butter and oil in a large pan and add the onions, garlic, shallots, and bay leaf. Cook over medium heat until the onions begin to caramelize. Add the salt and pepper, and continue to brown, stirring often. When browned, add the brandy and Madeira and cook until the liquid is almost gone. Add the wine, and cook until the liquids are reduced by half. Add both stocks and simmer for 30 minutes. Adjust the seasoning and remove the bay leaf.

To serve, ladle the soup into bowls, float a crouton on top, and sprinkle with about 3 tablespoons of cheese per serving. Put the bowls of soup on a baking sheet, place under a broiler, and broil until the cheese is lightly browned and bubbling.

Cream of Mushroom Soup

You're in luck if you live by a woods and are knowledgeable enough
to safely hunt for your own wild mushrooms—otherwise, best to be off to the store.
I prefer to use two or three different kinds of fresh mushrooms
because this gives the soup a more complex flavor. If you can't find a variety of fresh
mushrooms, you can substitute some dried ones for a portion of the amount
called for, or just make the soup with whatever mushrooms you can find in the market.
This is a very rich and creamy soup, so plan to serve it with a plain
salad and a simple entrée, such as grilled poultry or fish. For lunch, it would be plenty
satisfying with just a salad and some bread.

SERVES 6 TO 8

1	pound assorted fresh mushrooms (cèpes, chanterelles, porcini, hedgehog, oyster, shiitake, or button mushrooms)
2	tablespoons unsalted butter or olive oil
1	medium onion, chopped
1	tablespoon mixed chopped fresh herbs such as chervil, thyme, and parsley
1	teaspoon toasted ground cumin seed
	Kosher or sea salt
	Freshly ground white pepper
¾	cup white wine
4	cups Chicken Stock (page 223) or Vegetable Stock (page 224)
1	medium potato, peeled and diced
1-2	tablespoons dry sherry or Madeira, or ½-1 tablespoon aged sherry vinegar
1	cup heavy cream
6-8	sprigs chervil or 3-4 teaspoons minced parsley

Clean and roughly chop the mushrooms. Melt the butter or heat the oil in a large pot, and over medium-low heat, stew the onion until tender. Add the mushrooms and cook gently, covered, for 8 to 10 minutes, stirring occasionally. Do not allow to brown. Add the herbs, cumin seed, salt, and pepper, and cook uncovered for 5 minutes. Add the white wine, and over medium heat reduce the liquid by half. Add the stock and potato, and cook until the potato is tender. Add the sherry, Madeira, or vinegar.

Purée the soup and strain it into a clean pot. Stir in the cream and bring the soup just to a boil. Serve garnished with the chervil sprigs or minced parsley.

Split Pea and Apple-Smoked Bacon Soup

This is my husband's favorite soup. It is also one of the few soups my
mom would make from scratch. She made it with ham, so
I used to figure that whenever you had ham, you'd have split pea soup
the next day. I like the flavor of apple-smoked bacon, but you
can substitute other kinds of bacon (or even ham) depending on what's
available in your area. This soup will separate when
left to sit, so be sure to stir it well before heating and serving it.

SERVES 6

1   pound green split peas
2   tablespoons olive oil
1   medium onion, diced
3   cloves garlic, finely minced
1   large carrot, diced
2   stalks celery, diced
8   cups Chicken Stock (page 223)
4   ounces apple-smoked bacon, diced
3   sprigs basil
2   sprigs thyme
    Kosher or sea salt
    Freshly ground pepper to taste
1   cup heavy cream (optional)

Wash the split peas and remove any stones. Heat the oil in a large pot, and sauté the onion and garlic over medium heat until tender, but not browned. Add the carrot and celery, and cook for 5 to 8 minutes until they begin to get tender; remove from heat. Remove and reserve half the vegetables.

Add the split peas, basil, and thyme and stock to the vegetables in the pot. Bring to a boil, reduce heat to very low, cover, and simmer for 1 to 1½ hours, until the split peas are tender.

In a sauté pan, cook the bacon over medium heat until crisp. Drain and reserve.

Purée the soup in batches, and strain if desired. (If leaving unstrained, remove the sprigs of basil and thyme.) Put the soup in a clean pot, add the reserved vegetables and bacon, and simmer until all the vegetables are tender. Add the salt, pepper, and cream and stir. (If you prefer, you can whip the cream and serve a dollop on top of each serving.) If desired, garnish with small toasted croutons (page 228).

Butternut Squash and White Bean Soup

This is a big batch of soup, but it tastes even better the next day,
so I'm building in some leftovers. You could use bacon,
ham ends, or pancetta in place of the ham hock. Other squash such
as delicata, kabocha, or pumpkin can be substituted
for the butternut squash.

SERVES 12 TO 15

8	ounces white beans
8	cups water
1	meaty ham hock (1 pound)
2	bay leaves
½	onion peeled and stuck with 1 whole clove
3	tablespoons olive oil
1½	cups minced onion
1½	cups diced leeks, white parts only
1½	stalks celery, diced
2	medium carrots, peeled and diced
4	cups peeled and diced butternut squash
	Kosher or sea salt
	Freshly ground white pepper
1	tablespoon chopped sage
1	tablespoon chopped thyme
4	tablespoons chopped parsley

Wash the beans and check them for stones. Soak the beans in water overnight, or boil them for 5 minutes and then soak for 1 hour. Drain beans, transfer to a pot, and add the ham hock, bay leaves, the onion stuck with a clove, and water to cover. Bring to a boil, lower heat to a simmer, and cook, skimming often, until the beans are tender. This will take about 1 hour or more, depending on the freshness of the beans. Remove and discard the bay leaf and onion. Remove the ham hock. Pull the meat from the bone; shred or chop meat, and reserve.

Heat the oil in a large pot and sauté the minced onion, leek, celery, and carrots over medium heat until tender. Add the sautéed vegetables and the squash to the soup, and simmer for 10 to 15 minutes, until the squash is tender. Add the reserved meat, sage, thyme, and 2 tablespoons parsley. Simmer for a further 30 minutes until the flavors are developed. Serve garnished with the remaining parsley.

Black Bean Soup

This is one of those comfortable meal-in-a-bowl soups you can
eat while you sit on the couch and watch a good movie.
Try it in the summertime, garnished with a thin slice of avocado,
a squeeze of lime, and a dollop of sour cream. The spices
will bring up your inner heat and fool you into feeling cooler.
Dried beans need to soak overnight.

SERVES 6

8   ounces dried black beans (or 2 15-ounce cans)
¼   cup olive oil
1   large onion, diced
2   carrots, peeled and chopped
4-5 cloves garlic, chopped
¼ - ½ jalapeño or serrano chile, minced
1   tablespoon toasted ground cumin seeds
½   teaspoon ground cardamom
2   bay leaves
1   dried ancho or guajillo chile, toasted and julienned, or ½ tablespoon pure chile powder, or 2 tablespoons Chile Paste (page 226)
1   cup white wine or beer
4   cups Vegetable Stock (page 224), or Chicken Stock (page 223)
    Kosher or sea salt
    Freshly ground pepper
    Sherry vinegar to taste
1½ teaspoons orange zest

Garnish:
½   avocado, diced
½   tomato, seeded and diced
¼   bunch cilantro sprigs, leaves only
    Lime wedges (optional)
    Sour cream (optional)

Wash the beans and check them for stones. Soak the beans in water overnight, or bring to a boil for 5 minutes, and then soak for 1 hour. Drain.

Heat the olive oil in a large pan and add the onion, carrots, garlic, and minced jalapeño. Stew over medium heat until tender but not browned. Add the cumin, cardamom, and bay leaves, and cook for 2 minutes. Add the julienned dry chile (or chile powder or Chile Paste) and wine, and reduce the liquid by half. Then add the soaked beans, stock, salt, and pepper. Bring to a boil, reduce heat to a simmer, and skim off the foam that rises. Cook until the beans and carrots are tender, about 1 to 2 hours, depending on the freshness of the beans, adding more water or stock if necessary. Remove the bay leaves.

This soup can be served as is, or, if you like it perfectly smooth, you can purée and strain it. Sometimes I purée half and add it back to the rest. In any case, as a final step, adjust seasoning and stir in the sherry vinegar and orange zest. Pour into bowls, garnish, and serve.

Lobster Gazpacho

I got the inspiration for this cold seafood soup on a trip to Japan.
It's seasoned with sake and Japanese tamari soy sauce, instead of the
usual lemon juice and vinegar. This is an extravagant soup—
something you'd serve on a special occasion. I think it's Bill Higgins's
favorite dish, so I'll dedicate it to him.
Be sure to use a high-quality, flavorful olive oil (this is
true whenever you use olive oil in a dish that will be served cold).
Other cooking suggestions: 1) If you can get them, use fresh
green coriander seeds rather than dried seeds, and grind them yourself.
2) This soup is probably best made in the summer, when vegetables
are at their peak. Besides, summer would be the time of year to
serve a cold soup. 3) You can substitute shrimp or crab for the lobster.

Serves 6

1	2- to 2½-pound lobster, or 2 smaller lobsters
1	quart Court Bouillon (page 224)

Broth:

1	46-ounce can tomato juice
¾	cup rice vinegar
2	tablespoons extra-virgin olive oil
¾	cup sake
1½	teaspoons tamari soy sauce
1	cup dry white wine
1	tablespoon plus 2 teaspoons ground fresh green coriander seeds (much less if you're using commercially ground dried coriander)
	Kosher or sea salt
	Freshly ground white pepper

Vegetables:

½	cup tender young green beans
½	cup sweet peas or sugar snap peas

2	Japanese cucumbers, peeled and sliced lengthwise, or 1 regular cucumber peeled, seeded, and finely diced
1	cup minced red bell pepper
1	tablespoon finely minced fresh lemon grass
1	cup diced, seeded red tomatoes
½	cup diced, seeded yellow tomatoes (use all red tomatoes if the yellow are unavailable)
2	jalapeño chiles, seeded and minced

Garnish:

1	tablespoon minced chives
5	tablespoons minced scallions or red onions
3	tablespoons minced cilantro
2	tablespoons minced basil

Cook the lobster in a boiling court bouillon for 8 to 12 minutes, depending on its size. Cool, then remove the meat from the shell and cut into ½-inch chunks (you should have around ¾ pound meat). Refrigerate.

Mix together all the broth ingredients and chill.

Cut the beans (and sugar snap peas, if you use them) into 1-inch lengths. Blanch the beans and peas in lightly salted boiling water for 1 minute. Remove them and rinse with cold water. Combine with the remaining vegetables and mix into the broth.

Combine the chives, scallions, cilantro, and basil, and set aside. To serve, divide the lobster equally between the bowls. Ladle the vegetable broth over the lobster, and sprinkle with some of the garnish.

Scallop Ceviche

Ceviches are of Latin American origin. They are made by
"cooking" raw seafood (rock cod or snapper or scallops) in fresh
citrus juice—usually lime juice. I like to use a combination
of citrus juices rather than pure lime juice; feel free to experiment
with the relative proportions. It is extremely important
to use only very fresh, juicy scallops.
Ceviche makes a good buffet item: serve it in a bowl with
fresh corn tortillas on the side for scooping.

SERVES 6 TO 8

1	pound very fresh bay scallops, or sea scallops
¼	cup fresh lime juice
¼	cup fresh orange juice
¼	cup fresh lemon juice
¼	cup minced green bell pepper
¼	cup minced red bell pepper
¼	cup minced yellow bell pepper
¼	cup minced red onion
⅓	cup minced cilantro leaves
½	teaspoon minced roasted, peeled, and seeded serrano chile
½	teaspoon minced roasted, peeled, and seeded jalapeño chile
1	large or 2 small tomatoes, peeled, seeded, and diced
1-2	drops Tabasco sauce, or to taste
¼	cup extra-virgin olive oil
	Kosher or sea salt
	Freshly ground pepper

Garnish:

1	lime cut into thin wedges
	Sprigs of cilantro
½	avocado, thinly sliced or diced

Cut the scallops in half and remove the muscle. Combine the citrus juices in a glass, ceramic, or stainless steel bowl, and marinate the scallops in the juices for at least 2 to 3 hours in the refrigerator. While the scallops are marinating, combine the other ingredients.

When the scallops are "cooked," gently mix them together with the remaining ingredients. Garnish each serving with a wedge of lime, a sprig of cilantro, and some avocado.

Manila Clam Chowder

I never cared much for clam chowder until about twenty years ago
when John Byrnes made it one night for my sister and me.
John is now my brother-in-law, and his chowder is still, for me, the
standard against which I measure all others. This one is
a little different, but I think he'd be pleased.
Because of the volume of clams in this recipe, it's best to make it
up in several small batches. Try it and you'll
find that it's really not hard to keep two pans going at once.

SERVES 6

4	dozen Manila clams or other small hard-shelled clams (about 3 pounds)
¾	cup julienned bacon
2	tablespoons unsalted butter
2	tablespoons minced shallots
1	medium leek, diced
1½	cups cooked and sliced Finger-ling potatoes, or peeled red potatoes
1½	cups Fish Stock or Chicken Stock (page 223)
½	teaspoon Tabasco sauce
	Kosher or sea salt
	Freshly ground white pepper
1½	cups heavy cream
1	tablespoon chopped parsley
1	tablespoon chopped chives
½	cup goldfish or oyster crackers

Scrub and drain the clams. Cook the bacon and drain off the fat. Melt the butter in a pan. Add bacon, shallots, and leek, and sauté over medium heat for 1 minute. Add clams and shake the pot, then add potatoes, stock, Tabasco, salt, and pepper. Cover and heat through, about 2 to 3 minutes, then add cream and parsley. Discard any clams that are not open. Correct the seasoning and divide the clams and broth between the bowls. Garnish each bowl with a sprinkling of chopped chives and 3 or 4 crackers.

Red Curry Mussel Stew

This is the dish that was featured in the Visa commercial that was shot at Fog City Diner in 1990. During the first week that the commercial aired, the demand for this stew was so great at the Diner that we just couldn't get enough mussels. We use the black Prince Edward Island mussels, which measure about 1 inch in length. You can use any small black mussels as a substitute. Because of the quantity of mussels, it is better to make this recipe in several small pans rather than in one large pot. You can make the seasoned broth in one pan, and ladle some of it out into one or two other pans to cook the mussels.

SERVES 6

4	dozen Prince Edward Island mussels or any small black mussels (about 2½ pounds)
2	tablespoons unsalted butter
2	large cloves garlic, minced
1	tablespoon peeled and grated ginger
¼	cup peeled and diced tomato
1	tablespoon Red Curry Paste (page 227, or buy it in Thai markets)
4	cups canned coconut milk
1	tablespoon chopped cilantro
6	sprigs cilantro, for garnish

Scrub the mussels well and trim off the beards. Melt the butter in a large saucepan, and sauté the garlic, ginger, and tomato for 2 minutes. Add the curry paste and coconut milk, stirring until the paste dissolves. Add the mussels, cover, and steam until open, about 3 to 6 minutes (discard any mussels that do not open). Add the chopped cilantro; divide the mussels and broth between the bowls and garnish with sprigs of cilantro.

Duck Stew

This stew is Indonesian-inspired with a lot of not-so-everyday flavors.
It is somewhat spicy, but you can adjust the recipe to suit your
own taste. If you can get them in your area, use the Muscovy duck
breasts. They are quite large and work well in this dish.
It will improve the appearance of the dish if you cut the vegetables
into uniform ½-inch dice.

SERVES 6

2	ducks (or 2 Muscovy duck breasts)
3	tablespoons olive oil
½	large white onion, sliced
2	cloves garlic, minced
1	red bell pepper, diced
1	fresh poblano or pasilla chile, diced (or 2 jalapeños, seeded and diced)
1	large carrot, diced
2½	cups sweet potatoes or yams, peeled and cut into ½-inch dice
3	cups Chicken Stock (page 223), or stock made from the duck carcasses
1	teaspoon ground cumin
1	teaspoon ground coriander
1	teaspoon curry powder
½	teaspoon chile flakes, or to taste
	Kosher or sea salt
	Freshly ground pepper
½	cup coconut milk (optional)
1	large tomato, diced
2	cups cooked basmati rice
1½	tablespoons julienned fresh basil, for garnish
1½	tablespoons julienned fresh mint, plus whole leaves for garnish

Bone and skin the duck, and cut it into 1½-inch pieces. In a large skillet, heat half of the olive oil and brown the duck. Remove from the pan and reserve.

In a large sauté pan heat the remaining olive oil and sauté the onion and garlic until they are translucent. Add the bell pepper and chile and cook until tender. Add the carrot and sweet potatoes and cook until they are glazed with the olive oil, about 1 minute. Add the stock, spices, salt, and pepper, and cook until tender, about 12 minutes. Add the duck meat, coconut milk, tomatoes, and 1 tablespoon each of basil and mint. Cook 5 to 10 minutes longer, until the sauce has thickened.

Serve over steamed rice, garnished with the remaining mint and basil.

Sirloin and Black Bean Chili

This recipe makes a really thick hearty chili. For one thing, we use a cut of beef that
doesn't quickly dissolve into shreds. And then we thicken the chili with a
little masa harina, a flour made from finely ground, dried corn. The masa gives this dish
a more interesting flavor than regular flour would, but if you can't get masa,
a mixture of cornmeal and regular flour will also work. One time at home when I didn't have
any masa harina, I used shredded stale corn tortillas to thicken the chili,
and it worked very well. To give the dish a richer flavor, I like to use an assortment of pure
chile powders rather than just one kind. You can find them in Hispanic markets
(or look in the ethnic foods section in your local market). You can
serve the chili with steamed rice, or with Jalapeño Corn Stix (page 28) or fresh
Flour Tortillas (page 30). This chili is the base for our chili dogs.

SERVES 6

8	ounces (1¼ cups) dried black beans
4	cups water
3	tablespoons peanut oil or olive oil
1½	pounds sirloin, top or bottom round, trimmed of fat, cut into ½-inch by 1- to 2-inch chunks
2-4	cloves garlic, minced
2	medium onions, diced
1-3	jalapeño chiles, minced
⅓	cup masa harina
⅓	cup ancho chile powder, or pure New Mexico or Anaheim chile powder (or a combination)
2	bay leaves
½-1	teaspoon cayenne powder
1	teaspoon cumin, toasted and ground
4	cups Chicken Stock (page 223), or Veal Stock (page 222)
4-6	tablespoons Chile Paste (page 226), optional
	Kosher or sea salt to taste
	Fresly ground pepper to taste

Garnish:

6-8	ounces grated white cheddar or Monterey jack cheese
4	tablespoons minced sweet red onion or scallions
6-12	sprigs cilantro or chopped chives

Wash the beans and check them for stones. Soak the beans in water overnight. Drain, and place them in a pot with 4 cups water. Bring to a boil, turn off the heat, skim off any foam, and let sit for 30 minutes. Return the pot to a boil, reduce the heat, and simmer for 30 to 40 minutes or until the beans are tender. As the beans are cooking, add more water if necessary to keep them suspended. Drain, and reserve.

Heat 2 tablespoons of the oil in a large pot, and brown the meat in batches so that it doesn't steam in its own juices but is allowed to caramelize. Remove the meat and set it aside. Using the same pot, heat the remaining tablespoon of oil and sauté the garlic, onions, and chiles until tender, about 8 to 10 minutes. Add the masa harina, chile powder, bay leaves, cayenne, and cumin. Cook, stirring, for 3 to 5 minutes. Add the reserved meat, stock, and optional Chile Paste. Cook for a further 20 to 30 minutes, until the meat is tender and the flavors are melded. Add the beans, salt, and pepper and cook until hot throughout and thick. If it becomes too thick, add stock or water to thin. Remove the bay leaves before serving. Serve the chili sprinkled with cheese, red onions, and cilantro.

SMALL

CHAP

PLATES

TER 3

SMALL PLATES

CHAPTER 3

When we were planning our first menu and trying to figure out what to call this section, "Boo" said he didn't like the word "starters" because it was too trendy, and he didn't like the word "appetizers" either—that was too stuffy. In the end, we settled on "small plates." The nice thing about small plates is that they are so flexible. Some people stick with tradition and order one small plate as an appetizer before their main meal. Others will order two different ones and a salad or soup and skip the entrée. My favorite way of eating out is to bring along at least four other people with me so we can order a lot of different appetizers to share, and maybe split an entrée or two, and still have room for dessert. The recipe portions as given in this section are for one small plate per person. However, you could arrange all the food on one platter and let people help themselves, or you could double or even triple a recipe and use it as the main course. If you want to serve two or three different small plates at the same time, you should cut each recipe in half. There are no hard and fast rules—so be creative in your menu planning.

This was one of the very first dishes developed for the Fog City Diner. We wanted something unusual enough to spark the interest of our new customers, and tasty enough for them to spread the word around after trying it. We came up with this smooth, rich custard that has a subtle, sweet, garlic taste (because the garlic is cooked slowly, it loses all its bite). The custards should be served warm. You can make them several hours ahead of time (even a day ahead), and when you're ready to serve them, reheat them by setting the ramekins in a water bath while you prepare the sauce. For the sauce, you can use whatever variety of fresh mushrooms you can find—in the spring, morels would be great. A combination of mushrooms will give the sauce a more complex taste, and a greater depth of flavor.

SERVES 6 TO 8

Custard:

½   cup (about 15) peeled garlic cloves
2   cups cream
4   egg yolks
     Pinch of freshly grated nutmeg
     Kosher or sea salt
     Freshly ground white pepper

Sauce:

4   tablespoons butter
1   large clove garlic, minced
12   ounces mixed fresh mushrooms (such as chanterelles, shiitakes, morels, cremini, and porcini), sliced
3   cups Chicken Stock (page 223)
     Kosher or sea salt
     Freshly ground white pepper
1½-2 cups seasoned walnuts (page 228)
2   teaspoons minced chives

Place the garlic cloves in a small pan with 1 cup of water. Bring to a boil, drain, and repeat once more. Transfer the blanched garlic to a large pan, add the cream, and bring to a boil. Reduce heat to medium, and stirring occasionally, cook the mixture until it is thick enough to coat a spoon. Mash the mixture through a sieve or run it through a food mill using a fine disc (do not use a blender or processor, as they tend to aerate the mixture too much). Cool slightly. Meanwhile, preheat the oven to 250 degrees, start heating water for the water bath, and butter six 1½- or 2-inch ramekins.

Gently whisk the egg yolks into the garlic cream, and strain again through a fine sieve. Season with nutmeg, salt, and pepper. Pour the mixture into the prepared ramekins, and place them in a water bath with enough hot water to reach three-fourths the way up the side of the ramekins. Cover the ramekins with buttered parchment paper and then cover the entire water bath with foil. Bake at 250 degrees for about 30 to 40 minutes, or until set (an inserted knife tip should come out cleanly).

To prepare the sauce, melt 2 tablespoons of the butter in a pan and sauté the garlic and mushrooms over medium heat until tender. Add the stock, and reduce the mixture over medium heat until thickened. Add the remaining butter and season to taste with salt and pepper. Just before serving add the seasoned walnuts.

To serve, run a knife around edge of each ramekin to release the custard. Turn it out onto the center of the plate. Surround with hot mushroom sauce and garnish with minced chives. (Note: An easy way to mince chives is to snip them with scissors.)

I love chiles rellenos, the cheese-stuffed chiles that are dipped in an egg batter and fried, but I thought that a lighter and less caloric version would be even better, and that is how this recipe evolved. We stuff the chiles with a combination of cheeses—this blend gives the dish a more interesting flavor than a single cheese would, but you can adjust the combination to your own taste. This dish makes a nice centerpiece or focal point for a vegetarian meal.

SERVES 6

6	fresh pasilla (poblano) chiles, or Anaheims or pimentos
½	cup grated fontina cheese
½	cup grated Monterey jack cheese
½	cup grated Jarlsberg cheese
1	cup grated white cheddar cheese
½	cup grated asiago or parmesan cheese
	Avocado Salsa (recipe follows)
12	cilantro sprigs

Prepare the chiles by cutting all the way around the stem so that you can remove the stem and seed base in one piece. Keeping the stem and top intact, trim off any seeds and membranes, and if any get left behind in the pepper, remove them, too. Blanch the chiles for 2 minutes in lightly salted boiling water. Remove the chiles, refresh in ice water, and drain.

Combine the grated cheeses in a bowl and mix well. Stuff each chile with about ½ cup of the cheese mixture. Do not overstuff or pack the cheese in too densely. Replace the stem and top of the chile.

Cook on a grill over a medium fire, turning frequently until the cheeses are melted and the chiles are hot all the way through. Place on a bed of Avocado Salsa and garnish with the cilantro sprigs.

Avocado Salsa

This salsa also goes well with quesadillas and burgers—or just serve it with chips.

2	ripe avocados
½-1	jalapeño chile, roasted, seeded, and minced
½	small red onion, minced
3	scallions, minced (white part and 2 inches of green)
3	tablespoons roughly chopped cilantro
2	tablespoons rice vinegar
6	tablespoons olive oil
	Kosher or sea salt
	Freshly ground pepper

Cut each avocado in half. Remove the seed, make dice-sized criss-crosses in the avocado flesh with a knife, and scoop out the dice with a spoon. Place in a mixing bowl and add the chile, onion, scallions, and chopped cilantro. Whisk together the vinegar and oil in a separate bowl, add salt and pepper to taste, and pour over the avocado mixture. Mix gently, being careful not to mash the avocado or the salsa will look like guacamole and taste "muddy."

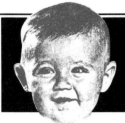

Quesadillas with Hazelnuts and Tomatillo Salsa

A quesadilla is a sort of grilled cheese sandwich made with flour tortillas instead of bread. Ours are homemade, and each one is large enough for two or three people depending on how many other items you are serving. We cut them into six wedge-shaped pieces. I've never met anyone who has actually eaten a whole quesadilla by themselves; someone else at the table usually grabs at least one wedge. Most of the waiters at the Diner recommend a side order of Avocado Salsa (see page 61) to go with the quesadillas.

SERVES 6

6   Flour Tortillas (page 30)
½   cup grated white cheddar
½   cup grated Monterey jack cheese
½   cup grated Jarlsberg cheese
½   cup grated fontina cheese
¼   cup grated asiago cheese
½   jalapeño chile, roasted and minced
3   scallions, minced
6   tablespoons chopped roasted hazelnuts
    Kosher or sea salt
    Freshly ground white pepper
    Tomatillo Salsa (recipe follows)
¼   cup chopped cilantro sprigs

Have the tortillas ready for assembling the quesadillas. In a mixing bowl, combine the cheeses, jalapeño, scallions, and hazelnuts, and season with salt and pepper. Sprinkle the mixture over 3 of the tortillas and cover each one with another tortilla to make a "sandwich." Heat the griddle or a pan over medium heat (do not add oil to the griddle), and cook the quesadillas on one side until the cheeses begin to melt. Turn them over to finish the other side— the melted cheese helps to hold them together. The tortillas should be golden brown and crisp on the outside.

To serve, cut each quesadilla into 6 wedges, and garnish at the center with 2 tablespoons of Tomatillo Salsa and some cilantro sprigs. Serve with additional salsa on the side.

Tomatillo Salsa

Tomatillos are a small round fruit that is enclosed in a papery brown husk. When the husk is removed, they look like small green tomatoes. Tomatillos are used a lot in Mexican cooking. If you can get seeds, try growing them. They grow like weeds here in Northern California. Green or red tomatoes can be substituted if you're unable to get tomatillos. This salsa also goes well with scrambled eggs, tortilla chips, and grilled fish.

24   medium tomatillos
1   teaspoon freshly ground toasted cumin seeds
2   tablespoons chopped cilantro
3   tablespoons red bell pepper, cut into ¼-inch dice
3   tablespoons red onion, cut into ¼-inch dice
1   tablespoon minced mint
    Kosher or sea salt
    Freshly ground white pepper

Peel the papery outer skin off the tomatillos. Roast them in a 375-degree oven for 15 to 20 minutes, until they begin to brown and are tender. You can also grill them, which gives the salsa a nice smoky background flavor. Place the roasted tomatillos, cumin, and cilantro in a blender or processor and purée until smooth. Transfer to a bowl, add the remaining ingredients, and mix well. Refrigerate.

Onion Rings

The only reason I am glad my stepdaughter Kirstie isn't in town with me
a lot is that when we're together, we always eat these, and I
can't burn them off like she does. Some say the Diner has the best onion rings
in town. One of our secrets is to prepare each one individually.
I don't know how many people actually deep-fry at home, but these onion rings
are certainly worth the effort. They're good with steaks or chops,
sandwiches or soups, or all by themselves. Of course you'll want to serve
them with Housemade Ketchup (page 168).

SERVES 6

5	large yellow onions
1	cup flour
1	cup water
1	teaspoon cayenne
1	teaspoon kosher or sea salt
1	teaspoon fresh cracked pepper
2	egg whites, beaten to soft peaks
2	cups fine bread crumbs

Peanut oil for frying

Peel the onions, being careful to remove all the dry papery skin, and cut them into ½-inch-thick slices. Only use the large outer rings, reserving the small inner rings for another use.

In a deep bowl, combine the flour, water, cayenne, salt, and pepper, and mix thoroughly. Fold in the beaten egg whites gently until the batter is light and fluffy. The bread crumbs need to be very, very fine: if necessary, put them through a fine sieve, and then into a wide container that's good for dipping.

Hook an onion ring on your finger and dip it in the batter, shaking off the excess. Dip it into the bread crumbs, coat thoroughly, and shake off excess. Place the breaded onion rings on a cookie sheet. When you run out of room, you can layer them up, separating each layer with parchment or waxed paper.

In a deep-fryer, heat the oil to 375 degrees and fry for 2½ minutes. If you do not have a deep-fryer, heat the peanut oil in a cast-iron skillet and fry the rings, turning them as necessary until golden brown and crisp.

We offer this as a small plate at the Diner, but it would make a good entrée for a vegetarian meal. You could also serve it as a side dish with grilled poultry or meat: whenever you have the barbecue all fired up, it's nice to use it for more than just one thing. The sauce can be made ahead.

SERVES 6

6   small Japanese eggplants, or 3 medium-small regular eggplants
2   red onions
⅓   cup olive oil
1   teaspoon kosher or sea salt
    Freshly ground pepper

Red Pepper Vinaigrette:

2   red bell peppers or 3-4 pimento peppers
3   tablespoons balsamic vinegar
2   cloves garlic, minced
    Kosher or sea salt
    Freshly ground pepper
9   tablespoons virgin olive oil
2   tablespoons minced chives or scallions

6-8 large mint leaves cut into chiffonade
6-12 sprigs cilantro
2   teaspoons scallions, finely sliced on the bias

If you're using Japanese eggplants, cut them in half lengthwise and crosshatch the cut sides with diagonal slash marks three-fourths of the way through the flesh; do not cut through the skin. This will make the eggplants grill more evenly. Cut standard eggplants into ½-inch-thick slices (you need 12 slices, 2 per person). Peel the onions and slice them ¼ inch thick. Coat the onions and the cut sides of the eggplants thoroughly with oil, and season with salt and pepper. Set aside.

To prepare the sauce, grill or broil the red bell peppers or pimentos over medium heat until blackened on all sides. Transfer to a large bowl and cover bowl with plastic wrap. Let the peppers sweat, and when they are cool, peel, seed, and stem them. Then mince them finely and reserve. Combine the vinegar, garlic, salt, and pepper, and whisk in the oil to emulsify it. Stir in the peppers. Transfer the sauce to a bowl, and add the chives.

Grill the eggplants and onions for 3 to 5 minutes over medium-high heat until cooked through and tender, brushing with additional oil if necessary. The onions should be caramelized.

To serve, arrange 2 eggplant halves (or 2 slices of regular eggplant) and 2 slices of red onion alternately on a plate. Spoon the sauce in a line down the center. In a bowl, combine the mint, cilantro, and scallions, and sprinkle over the eggplant.

Baked Buffalo Mozzarella with Pesto on Toast

The buffaloes involved in making this dish are not American, they're Italian.
Originally mozzarella came from the south of Italy and was
made from water buffalo milk. There are several American cheese makers
who make mozzarella from cow's milk, and you can use this type
if you can't find buffalo mozzarella, although there will be some difference in
texture and in the way the cheese melts. Whatever you do, don't use
ultraprocessed rubbery mozzarella. Many gourmet stores or cheese shops will
have either the Italian mozzarella, which comes in oval-shaped balls
weighing about 4 or 5 ounces each, or a good local product.

SERVES 6

3-4   rounds fresh buffalo mozzarella
      cheese (about 1 pound in all)
¼   cup olive oil
      Freshly ground white pepper
1   large red bell pepper
1   large yellow bell pepper
12   Croutons (page 228)
½   cup Pesto (page 166)

Cut the mozzarella into 12 slices, ¼ to ⅓ inch thick, and place on a large plate or in a bowl so that each slice is separated from the others. Pour the olive oil over the cheese, making sure each slice is lightly coated with the oil. Sprinkle with pepper, and marinate in the refrigerator until you are ready to use it.

On a grill or under the broiler, roast the bell peppers until the skins are blackened all over. Transfer to a bowl and cover bowl with plastic wrap. Let sweat, and when cool, peel, seed, and cut each pepper lengthwise into 6 strips.

Preheat the oven to 375 to 425 degrees. Place the croutons on an ovenproof serving plate, and top each one with a slice of mozzarella. Bake for 2 to 3 minutes until the cheese just begins to melt. Garnish each round with 2 crossed strips of roasted bell peppers and drizzle pesto over the center. Serve 2 croutons per person.

Mustards Grill's Goat Cheese Toast

This popular appetizer originated at Mustards Grill, our Napa Valley restaurant. We use a crusty oval sourdough loaf for the croutons, but any good-quality French or Italian-style baguette will do fine. We serve this at the Diner on special occasions (it's great for parties).

8	ounces fresh goat cheese (Laura Chenel's Chèvre Chabis)
8	tablespoons heavy cream or Crème Fraîche (page 169)
2	minced shallots
1	tablespoon Dijon mustard
2	tablespoons dry sherry vinegar or balsamic vinegar
	Pinch of salt
6	tablespoons light olive oil
12	Croutons (page 228)
1	tablespoon cracked black peppercorns
6	sun-dried tomatoes, cut into lengthwise pieces
6	tablespoons chiffonade of basil

In a mixing bowl, mix the goat cheese and cream or crème fraîche together with a wooden spoon until it reaches a spreading consistency. Do not chill. To make the vinaigrette, combine the shallots, mustard, vinegar, and salt in another bowl. Gradually whisk in the oil, and continue whisking until emulsified.

Spread the croutons with the goat cheese mixture. Return the croutons to the broiler and broil just until the cheese is warm. Place the croutons on a serving plate. Drizzle a little bit of vinaigrette over the cheese, sprinkle with cracked peppercorns, and top with pieces of sun-dried tomato and a little basil.

You only need a bit of vinaigrette per toast—any leftover is great with a mixed green salad.

Mushroom Toast

To turn this small plate into a nice supper, add a green salad and a good bottle of wine. It's romantic food; best eaten in front of a fire on a stormy night, with all thoughts of diet and cholesterol thrown to the winds.

4	tablespoons unsalted butter
2	shallots, peeled and minced
¼	pound chanterelles or morels, roughly chopped
¼	pound shiitakes, stemmed and roughly chopped
¼	pound button mushrooms, sliced into large circles
2	teaspoons minced fresh thyme
1¼	cups Madeira
½	cup Chicken Stock (page 223)
1	cup heavy cream
	Kosher or sea salt
	Freshly ground black pepper
	Freshly grated nutmeg to taste
12	Croutons made from egg bread or from the Cheese Bun dough baked into loaves (page 19)
2	tablespoons minced chives

In a large saucepan, heat the butter over medium heat until it begins to bubble. Add the shallots and cook over medium heat for 1 to 2 minutes: do not let them brown. Add the mushrooms and sauté until caramelized and their juices have been released, 2 to 3 minutes. Add the thyme. Add the Madeira and reduce until the liquid has almost all evaporated. Add the chicken stock, bring to a boil, and reduce by half. Stir in the cream and season with salt, pepper, and nutmeg. Reduce further until thick enough to coat the back of a spoon.

To serve, place 2 croutons on each plate and top with the mushroom mixture. Sprinkle with chives.

Seared Rare Tuna, Japanese-Style

Sometime in the mid to late '80s, when the song "Turning Japanese"
was popular, and San Francisco had gone from Cajun blackened everything
to sushi/sashimi mania, we created this dish. We use loins from
the tail portion of the tuna, because when they are sliced across the grain,
you get neat 2-inch triangles that make perfect serving-sized pieces.
If you can't get this particular cut, use a tuna fillet, and do your best to cut
it up neatly after it is grilled. Wasabi is Japanese horseradish:
you can buy the powder in oriental markets.

SERVES 6 TO 8

1	pound tuna fillet
2	tablespoons tamari soy sauce
2	tablespoons olive oil
1	teaspoon peeled and grated ginger
2	teaspoons minced shallots
½	cup Pickled Ginger (page 168)
	Wasabi Drizzle, Chinese Mustard Drizzle, and Soy Drizzle (recipes follows)
	Kosher or sea salt
	Coarsely ground black pepper
2	scallions, thinly sliced on the bias
	Fresh chervil leaves
2	tablespoons sesame seeds, toasted
2	cups arugula, small leaves (optional)
2	cups small red mustard greens or watercress (optional)

Remove the skin from the tuna fillet. Combine the soy sauce, olive oil, ginger, and shallots in a mixing bowl. Add the tuna and marinate for about ½ hour in the refrigerator. Remove tuna from marinade; heat a cast-iron pan and quickly sear the tuna on each side. You can also grill it over medium-high heat until nicely caramelized, but still rare on the inside, about 5 to 7 minutes.

Slice the tuna a bit thicker than ¼ inch. For each serving, place 3 slices of tuna slightly overlapping down the center of a small oval plate with Pickled Ginger at one end. Drizzle with the three drizzle sauces and sprinkle with salt and pepper. Garnish with scallions, chervil, and sesame seeds.

To make into an entrée salad, mix arugula and Japanese red mustard greens and toss lightly in a simple rice vinegar vinaigrette (page 79) and serve with a few greens under the tuna and alongside it. For a buffet this also looks good with the slices arranged on a large oval platter, and the greens arranged around the tuna.

Wasabi Drizzle

2	tablespoons wasabi
3	tablespoons rice vinegar
2	tablespoons half-and-half

Mix the wasabi and rice vinegar together and let sit 10 to 20 minutes. Add the half-and-half and stir well.

Chinese Mustard Drizzle

3	tablespoons Chinese Mustard (page 169)
1	tablespoon rice vinegar to thin
1	tablespoon olive oil

Combine and set aside.

Soy Drizzle

2	tablespoons virgin olive oil
1	tablespoon tamari soy sauce

Mix well just before using.

Asian-Style Sautéed Prawns with Pickled Ginger

SERVES 6 TO 8

The fish sauce, lemon grass, hoisin sauce, and black bean chile paste give this dish its distinctive Asian taste. All are available from Asian markets and specialty food stores. The sauce, which is very sweet and hot, adds succulence to the prawns.

1   pound small prawns (about 35)
      Kosher or sea salt
      Freshly ground pepper

Sauce:

1   3-inch piece of lemon grass (bulb end), finely chopped
2   tablespoons Vietnamese or Thai fish sauce
6   tablespoons honey
6   tablespoons hoisin sauce
2   tablespoons Chile Paste (page 226)
2   teaspoons black bean chile paste or black bean paste with garlic

2   tablespoons peanut oil
1   tablespoon white wine
      Pickled Ginger (page 168)
3   scallions, finely sliced on the bias

Peel and devein the prawns, and sprinkle with a little salt and pepper. Combine the sauce ingredients in a bowl, mix well, and reserve. Heat the oil, and sauté the prawns until half cooked, about 1 minute. Add the wine and bring it to a boil; add the sauce and simmer, stirring or tossing to coat the prawns, until the prawns are cooked through. If it's easier, you can sauté the prawns in two or three batches, throw all the prawns back in the pan, and finish the sauce. Top each serving with a few slices of Pickled Ginger and a sprinkling of scallions.

Chilled Prawns with Chinese Mustard and Crème Fraîche

SERVES 6 TO 8

Serve these prawns along with the Dungeness crab and oysters on the half shell for a great beginning to a dinner party. There's very little preparation involved, and most of it can be done ahead of time. You don't even need to peel the prawns before cooking them: in fact, they taste better when they're cooked in the shell. You and your guests will then have the fun of peeling the prawns as you eat them (be sure to provide plates for the shells, napkins, and lemon wedges). You can use the court bouillon for poaching any type of shellfish. This becomes the classic shrimp cocktail if you serve the prawns with the cocktail sauce (see next recipe).

2   pounds small prawns (approximately 70)
      Court Bouillon (page 224)
1   cup Chinese Mustard (page 169)
1   cup Crème Fraîche (page 169), or sour cream
      Lemon wedges

Rinse the prawns under cold water. Bring the court bouillon to a boil. Add the prawns and cook for 3 to 5 minutes, until just cooked. Drain the prawns and allow them to cool.

Mix the Chinese Mustard and Crème Fraîche together, and serve it with the prawns.

Oysters on the Half Shell with Housemade Cocktail Sauce

As you walk in Fog City Diner, you will see the oyster bar displaying mussels, cold cooked prawns, crayfish, crab or lobster, when they're in season, and at least three different kinds of oysters. Oysters are by far the most popular of all the items we offer. We serve our housemade cocktail sauce with them; the sauce is also good for prawns and crab. If you can get several different kinds of oysters, it's fun to compare them. My favorite variety is the tiny Olympia—you can eat a lot of those. But for most kinds of oysters you should plan on six per person. Diner White Bread with Dutch Crunch Topping (pages 17–18) or a baguette, the cocktail sauce, and lots of lemon are all you need to serve with the oysters—that and a glass of good white wine or your favorite beer.

SERVES 6

36 fresh oysters, scrubbed
Lemon wedges for garnish
Tabasco sauce to taste
Freshly grated horseradish to taste

Cocktail Sauce:

1¼ cups Heinz ketchup
2½ tablespoons finely grated fresh horseradish
Juice of ½ lemon
¾ teaspoon Tabasco sauce
1 teaspoon Worcestershire sauce
Pinch of kosher or sea salt
Pinch of freshly ground white pepper

Have ready a large serving platter covered with a layer of crushed ice. Shuck the oysters carefully with an oyster knife, protecting your hand with a towel. Detach the oysters from the shells, leaving them contained in the deepest half shells with as much oyster liquid as possible. Check for shell fragments, and remove any that you find. Place the oysters on the bed of ice.

To prepare the cocktail sauce, thoroughly combine all the sauce ingredients in a mixing bowl.

Serve with the cocktail sauce, plenty of lemon wedges, and additional Tabasco sauce and horseradish for those who like their food a little spicier.

We use Dungeness crab, which comes from Pacific Coast waters,
but if you can't get it, blue crab is a very good substitute.
Use whatever is available in your area. It's important to use live
crab because then you can be sure the crab is really fresh.
Not only that, so often when you buy cooked crab, it will be too salty.
Even though you are going to split and crack the crab
beforehand, it is going to be a little messy to eat. You might want
to provide nutcrackers, extra napkins, bibs, and plates for
the shells. The Dill and Scallion Mayonnaise will go well with
any fish, and it's also good for tuna salad sandwiches.

SERVES 6

3   live Dungeness crabs, each
       about 2-2½ pounds
       Court Bouillon (page 224)

Dill and Scallion Mayonnaise:

1½   cups mayonnaise (page 169)
1½-2 tablespoons minced fresh dill
2   scallions, minced

Bring the court bouillon to a boil and add the crabs. (The crabs need to be totally immersed, so you may need to cook them one at a time. You could also add a little water to the court bouillon to bring the level up.) Return the pot to a boil, and cook for 7 minutes per pound. If the meat is still translucent, cook for 2 minutes more.

Combine the mayonnaise, dill, and scallions and mix thoroughly. Keep refrigerated.

Remove the crabs from the pot, and allow to cool. When cool enough to handle, snap off the top shell and remove the gills and orange matter from the body of the crab. Split the body in half and cut each half in thirds again (6 pieces total for each crab). Break the legs from the body and crack them. Serve the crabs hot or cold, with the Dill and Scallion Mayonnaise in a ramekin on the side.

Note: Cocktail Sauce (page 71) and drawn butter could also accompany the crab. You can offer these in addition to the Dill and Scallion Mayonnaise and let your guests choose their favorite dip.

Crab Cakes with Sherry-Cayenne Mayonnaise

Not only is this Terry Higgins's favorite dish, but it seems to be everyone else's favorite, as well. This is the single most popular item at the Diner, and I can't even begin to imagine how much crabmeat we must have gone through since we opened. The Sherry-Cayenne Mayonnaise makes a great dipping sauce. You could also serve it with steamed lobster, or use it as a nonclassic Louis sauce.

Serves 8 to 10

Crab Cakes:

2	pounds crabmeat (preferably blue crab)
¼	cup minced red bell pepper
¼	cup minced green bell pepper
¼	cup minced yellow bell pepper
1-1½	inner stalks of celery, including leaves, minced
¼	cup minced sweet red onion
½	jalapeño chile, seeded and minced
2	large eggs
1	tablespoon Tabasco sauce
1½	teaspoons Worcestershire sauce
½	cup mayonnaise (page 169)
½-¾	cup fine bread crumbs

Sherry-Cayenne Mayonnaise:

1	cup mayonnaise (page 169)
1	teaspoon cayenne
2	tablespoons sherry vinegar
	Peanut oil for deep-frying
8-10	lemon wedges

Check the crabmeat for pieces of shell and gently squeeze out any excess moisture. Do not break up the larger pieces of meat, as these enhance the texture of the crab cakes. In a large bowl, combine all the crab cake ingredients, mixing well but lightly. Form into cakes about 2 inches in diameter and ½ inch high.

To prepare the Sherry-Cayenne Mayonnaise, mix 1 cup mayonnaise, cayenne, and vinegar together well. Keep refrigerated until needed.

Heat the oil to 375 degrees. Deep-fry the crab cakes for about 3 minutes, or until golden brown and crispy on the outside. The crab cakes can also be pan-fried, if you prefer.

Serve 3 crab cakes per person, and top each with 1½ to 2 teaspoons of Sherry-Cayenne Mayonnaise. Garnish each serving with a lemon wedge.

Spicy Scallops
with Chile Mayonnaise

Large sea scallops work best in this dish because they have a better flavor, and you can get them crispy on the outside without drying them out. The scallops are coated with a spicy breading, deep-fried, and served on a bed of lightly dressed cabbage. The cooking time is very short, so it's best to have the salad ready before you start frying the scallops. If you prefer not to deep-fry, the scallops can also be seared in a lightly oiled nonstick pan. This dish was developed by Pat Coll (Pat served as chef at the Diner while our regular chef, Robert, helped me open Roti).

SERVES 8

1¼   pounds sea scallops

Breading:

½   cup flour
½   cup cornmeal
1½   teaspoons paprika
¼   teaspoon cayenne powder
1½   teaspoons ground cumin
1½   teaspoons kosher or sea salt
1½   teaspoons freshly ground white pepper
1½   tablespoons pure chile powder

6   tablespoons olive oil
2   tablespoons rice vinegar
     Kosher or sea salt to taste
     Freshly ground pepper to taste
½   head red cabbage, thinly shredded
½   bunch scallions, cut on the bias
½   bunch cilantro, leaves only

Chile Mayonnaise:

¾   cup mayonnaise (page 169)
3½   tablespoons Chile Paste (page 226)
     Juice of 1 lemon
     About 2 tablespoons cold water

     Peanut oil for deep-frying
2   lemons, cut into wedges

Remove the connecting muscles from the sides of the scallops and check the scallops for shell fragments. Combine the breading ingredients in a bowl, mix well, and pass it through a sieve. Dust the scallops with a light, even coating, and shake off any excess.

Combine the oil, vinegar, salt, and pepper to make a vinaigrette. Toss the cabbage, scallions, and cilantro together in a bowl, and dress lightly with the vinaigrette.

To make the Chile Mayonnaise, combine the mayonnaise, Chile Paste, and lemon juice and mix well. Add water, using only as much as necessary to get a sauce that is relatively thick, yet thin enough to be drizzled.

Deep-fry the scallops for approximately 1 minute, or pan-fry them to medium-rare in a lightly oiled skillet. To serve, place the dressed cabbage on small plates, and top with the scallops. Drizzle with Chile Mayonnaise, and garnish with wedges of lemon.

As my partner Bill Upson says, if it's not broke don't fix it. We've been serving this dish at the Fog City Diner ever since we opened, and it's still as popular as ever. My husband is one faithful fan: he eats this together with a quesadilla 90 percent of the time when he comes to the Diner. It's a weird Southwest-Asian combo—but he likes it.

You can increase the recipe to a large plate size by doubling the marinade and using half a chicken breast per person. You don't even need to use skewers if you can handle grilling the chicken without them.

SERVES 6

1¼ pounds boned and skinned chicken breast

Marinade:

2 tablespoons sesame oil
1 tablespoon tahini (sesame seed paste)
1 tablespoon dark soy sauce
½ tablespoon light brown sugar
Juice of ¼ lemon
1-2 shakes Tabasco sauce
1 tablespoon ketjap manis (or 1 teaspoon molasses plus 2 teaspoons tamari or dark soy sauce)
2 tablespoons peeled and grated ginger
2 cloves garlic, minced

4 tablespoons unsalted butter
2 cups julienned carrots
2 tablespoons minced shallots
¼ pound shiitake mushrooms, julienned
¼ cup dry sherry vinegar
¼ cup rice vinegar
1½ cups Chicken Stock (page 223)
Kosher or sea salt
Freshly ground pepper
¼ cup Chinese Mustard (page 169)
2 tablespoons minced chives

Cut the chicken into 12 strips about ½ inch thick and 2 to 3 inches long. The easiest way to do this is to pull off the tenderloin (the piece of meat on the inside of each breast and closest to the bone) and cut the rest of the breast to the same size. Combine the marinade ingredients in a large mixing bowl. Marinate the chicken for at least 2 hours or as long as overnight.

Melt half the butter in a sauté pan or skillet. Add the carrots, shallots, and mushrooms, and sauté over medium heat until tender. Add the vinegars and reduce the liquid by about half. Add the stock and reduce the liquid again by half. Add the remaining butter and salt and pepper to taste.

While the sauce is reducing, remove the chicken from the marinade and thread it on skewers. Grill over a medium-hot to hot grill (or under a broiler) until done.

We serve the chicken on small oval plates: at one end we place a teaspoonful of Chinese Mustard, then we distribute the vegetables over the rest of the plate, pour the sauce over them, and top them with the grilled chicken and a sprinkling of chives.

Buffalo Chicken Wings with Stilton Bleu Cheese Dip

I believe these hot, spicy wings got their name from the city of Buffalo, New York, where the dish was invented. What makes Buffalo Wings unique is that they are always served with a bleu cheese dip. The dip is also great for big fat spears of asparagus or other vegetables, which can help balance out the couch-potato diet (for some reason I imagine people eating Buffalo Wings while they're sitting around at home watching football). There are many wonderful blue-veined cheeses: I happen to like Stilton, but you can use any other good bleu cheese. Bleu cheeses can get overripe, so it's wise to taste, or at least smell, before buying (if there's any scent of ammonia, keep looking).

SERVES 6

4½ pounds chicken wings
½ cup Tabasco sauce
1 tablespoon Worcestershire sauce
Peanut oil for deep-frying

Sauce:
3 tablespoons unsalted butter
2 tablespoons Tabasco sauce

Dip:
¾ cup mayonnaise (page 169)
⅓ cup sour cream
3 tablespoons minced jicama
4 tablespoons minced celery
2-3 drops Tabasco sauce
¼ pound Stilton cheese, crumbled
1 dash of Worcestershire sauce
1 tablespoon minced scallions
Freshly ground white pepper

Cut the wings into 3 pieces, and reserve the tips for stock. In a large mixing bowl, combine ½ cup Tabasco and 1 tablespoon Worcestershire sauce. Add the wings, toss to coat thoroughly, and marinate for 3 to 4 hours or as long as overnight.

Heat the peanut oil to 365 degrees and deep-fry the chicken wings for about 5 to 8 minutes, until browned and cooked through. Mix the sauce ingredients together in a large sauté pan. When the butter begins to bubble, toss in the wings to thoroughly coat them. You might want to do this in several batches.

If you prefer not to deep-fry the wings, place the marinated wings in a single layer in a roasting pan and bake at 450 degrees for 15 to 20 minutes, stirring occasionally until the skin is crispy. Heat the butter and 2 tablespoons Tabasco sauce in a saucepan and drizzle it over the baked wings, or serve the sauce alongside the wings with the Stilton dip. The chicken wings can also be barbecued over a grill or hibachi. Baste them with the butter-Tabasco sauce as they are grilling.

To prepare the Stilton dip, thoroughly combine the dip ingredients in a serving bowl. Chill.

Grilled Beef and Chanterelle Mushrooms with Arugula

You can thread the meat on skewers if you think it will be easier.
In the restaurant we don't even bother half the time. If you think you can
handle 18 separate pieces of meat on a hot grill, you don't
have to use them either. The sauce in this recipe is also good for
grilling any cut of steak, or chicken breasts or pork.

SERVES 6

1½ pounds beef sirloin or tender-loin

Basting Sauce:

1½-2 tablespoons finely minced lemon grass
2 cloves garlic, minced
½ tablespoon grated fresh ginger
4 tablespoons Dijon mustard
2 tablespoons rice vinegar
2 tablespoons olive oil
Pinch of freshly ground pepper

Salad:

3 cups arugula
½ cup cilantro sprigs, mostly leaves
2 large red or yellow tomatoes, peeled, seeded, and diced
1 shallot, peeled and minced
1 teaspoon minced lemon grass
1 small clove garlic, peeled and smashed
1 red serrano or jalapeño chile, julienned

Vinaigrette:

2 tablespoons rice vinegar
4 tablespoons light olive oil
2 tablespoons extra-virgin olive oil
Kosher or sea salt to taste
Freshly ground pepper to taste

1 pound chanterelle or shiitake mushrooms
3 tablespoons olive oil
Kosher or sea salt
Freshly ground pepper

Trim the meat of all fat and sinew, and cut it across the grain into 18 thin slices (or ask your butcher to do this for you). Combine all the sauce ingredients in a large mixing bowl and set aside.

Wash and dry the arugula and cilantro and combine in a large bowl with the tomatoes, shallot, lemon grass, garlic, and chile. Refrigerate until ready to serve. In a separate bowl, whisk together the vinaigrette ingredients. Set aside.

Clean the mushrooms thoroughly. Slice them in half if they are too large to handle for grilling, and if you are using shiitakes, remove the stems. Dress the mushrooms with half of the basting sauce, and the meat with the other half. Thread the mushrooms and meat on separate skewers (the mushrooms take longer to cook). When you thread the skewers, you want the meat and the mushroom caps to lie relatively flat so they will grill evenly and caramelize nicely. If you prefer, you can grill the mushrooms and slices of meat without skewering. Grill them over medium-hot fire, but be careful not to overcook.

Just before serving, toss the arugula with the vinaigrette. Arrange the mushrooms and meat alternately on a plate and sprinkle with the dressed greens and vegetables. Be careful not to completely cover up the grilled meat and mushrooms.

Marinated Pork Loin Satay with Mango Salsa

Satays are an Indonesian dish, small pieces of meat, poultry,
or seafood that have been marinated in a sweet, spicy marinade, then
skewered and grilled. They are commonly sold at street stalls
and cafés there, and are usually served with a spicy peanut sauce. But I like
the combination of pork and fruit better, not so much plain fresh
fruit, but fruit chutneys, relishes, and salsas, so at the Diner, we serve the pork
satay with Mango Salsa. Sambal oleck is an Indonesian chile
paste; ketjap manis is a heavy Indonesian soy sauce. If you can't get either
one, use the substitutes listed below.

SERVES 6 TO 8

2   pork tenderloins, 12 ounces to
     1 pound each

Marinade:

1   tablespoon peeled and grated
     ginger
3   cloves garlic, minced
1   tablespoon hoisin sauce
1   tablespoon sambal oleck (or
     black bean chile paste)
3   tablespoons ketjap manis (or 2
     tablespoons dark soy or tamari
     plus 1 tablespoon molasses)
½   teaspoon freshly ground white
     pepper
½   cup olive oil
½   bunch cilantro

Trim the tenderloins of all fat and
sinew, and cut them on the bias
into ¼-inch-thick slices. Combine
the marinade ingredients in a
large mixing bowl, and marinate
the pork slices for at least 2 hours
or preferably overnight.

Grill the pork slices (this
should go quickly as these are
thin pieces of meat). Place 3 slices
of meat on each plate, spoon
Mango Salsa in a line down the
center, and garnish with 3 or 4
nice sprigs of cilantro.

Mango Salsa

Don't prepare this in advance as
it doesn't keep well. This salsa is
also good with chicken or pork
chops.

1   mango, peeled, seeded, and
     diced
2   jalapeños, grilled, peeled, and
     minced
     Zest and juice of 2 limes
     Pinch each of sea salt and
     pepper
2   tablespoons extra-virgin olive
     oil

Gently mix all the ingredients
together in a bowl.

Grilled Sweetbreads with Lemon, Parsley, and Caper Butter

Because they are very perishable, it is hard to find fresh sweetbreads in the market, but it's worth the search. As soon as you get the sweetbreads home, blanch them as described below, and refrigerate them right away. The classic way of preparing sweetbreads is to sauté them, which, of course, you could do, but I think they are even better grilled. Grilled sweetbreads are slightly smoky and caramelized on the outside and rich and creamy in the center. A real treat! In this dish, the richness of the sweetbreads is cut by the tartness of the capers and lemon juice in the sauce.

Serves 6 to 8

1½   pounds veal sweetbreads
2   quarts cold water
    Juice of 1 lemon
2   tablespoons flour
2-3   sprigs parsley
1   tablespoon cracked black pepper

Marinade:

2   cloves garlic, peeled and minced
2   tablespoons mixed minced herbs (parsley, chervil, tarragon, basil, and/or fennel)
    Juice of 2 lemons
    Kosher or sea salt
    Freshly ground pepper
1½   tablespoons Dijon mustard
3   tablespoons olive oil

Lemon, Parsley, and Caper Butter:

½   cup unsalted butter
3   tablespoons minced shallots
    Juice of 1 lemon
5   tablespoons tiny capers, rinsed
5   tablespoons minced parsley

Put the sweetbreads in a large saucepan with enough cold water to cover by 1½ to 2 inches of water. Add the lemon juice, flour, parsley, and black pepper. Bring to a boil, reduce to a simmer, and cook for 8 to 12 minutes, keeping the sweetbreads covered by liquid at all times. Drain and cool, then remove the fat and membranes and cut the sweetbreads into 12 nice pieces. Combine all the marinade ingredients in a large mixing bowl. Add the cut sweetbreads to the marinade and place all in a pan with another pan or plate on top. Press under a light weight (a couple of boxes of pasta, for instance) and refrigerate for

2 hours. This cools and sets the sweetbreads.

Grill the sweetbread pieces over medium heat until caramelized and golden on all sides and hot all the way through. You may find it easier to manage all of the pieces if you put them on a skewer first.

To prepare the caper butter, heat the butter in a sauté pan over medium heat until it becomes hot and bubbly. Add the shallots and continue to cook until the butter begins to brown. Add the lemon juice and capers, and reduce a bit. Just before serving, toss in the parsley and swirl it about.

Arrange the sweetbreads on individual plates and spoon about 1½ to 2 tablespoons of the flavored butter over each serving.

SANDW

CHAP

ICHES

SANDWICHES
CHAPTER 4

This chapter should really have been written by my partners—they think I have no skill or aptitude for things in between bread. I think that's because I once told them that I love onion and radish sandwiches.   Over the years I've developed a few rules for successful sandwich making. First, make sure people can bite easily through the bread and filling without the rest of the sandwich landing in their laps. Second, slice the onions so thinly that even "Boo" and "Up" won't know they're there. And third, don't have any more than six sandwiches on the menu at once. That way we can cover all the bases by offering a fish sandwich, a vegetarian sandwich, a sandwich made with red meat, and one with poultry (plus the Diner Burger and the Diner Chili Dog). More or less something for everybody.

Diner Burger with Fries and Bread and Butter Pickles

We'll never sell as many burgers as McDonalds, but most Sunday
afternoons it feels like we're running a close second.

We serve a lot of nontraditional food at the Diner, but our burgers are about as
traditional as you can get. They're big, fat, and juicy.

Let's face it—if you're on a diet you'd be better off eating carrot sticks and celery.

When you buy ground beef, make sure that it is cleanly
cut and is bright red and white, not mushy and pink. The best burger meat
is a grade with 18 to 22 percent fat content.

Your doctor won't approve, but your taste buds will.

SERVES 6

2 pounds ground chuck
Kosher or sea salt
Freshly ground pepper
6 slices sharp cheddar cheese (optional)
6 Hamburger Buns (page 22)
6 leaves crisp romaine lettuce
12 thin slices tomato
6 thin slices red onion
French Fries (page 158)
Bread and Butter Pickles (page 167)

Season the ground beef with salt and pepper and divide it into 6 patties. We slap the patties back and forth to make sure they are solid, but not overly worked. If they're too loose, they'll fall apart before they're properly cooked; if they're handled too much or kneaded, they'll become tough and dry.

Cook on a medium-hot grill for about 5 minutes total for medium-rare or 7 to 8 minutes total for medium, turning once. Do not press down on the burgers while they're cooking or you'll squeeze out all the juices. For cheeseburgers, place the cheese slices on the burgers after turning them, so the cheese will melt by the time the burgers are done.

Split the hamburger buns and toast them on the grill or under the broiler. Place each burger on the bottom half of a bun, and put the top on at a slight angle so people can remove the top easily and put on the ketchup, mayonnaise, mustard, etc.

On each serving plate place a leaf of romaine lettuce, and then, in this order, a slice of tomato, a slice of onion, and another slice of tomato. Serve with fries, pickles, and plenty of ketchup, mustard, or whatever else you like on your burger. I like it with crisp bacon and Avocado Salsa (page 61), but of course, that's probably as bad for you as anything could possibly be.

Cheesesteak Sandwich

I have not been to Philadelphia to sample the real thing, but it sounded
like the kind of sandwich we should have at the Diner.
It was on our opening menu, and still appears now and then.
It's kind of messy to eat, so make sure you have plenty of napkins.

SERVES 6

3 tablespoons olive oil

2 medium onions, thinly sliced top to bottom

2 pounds top round, sliced paper-thin (have your butcher slice it for you)
Kosher or sea salt
Freshly ground pepper

1-1½ teaspoons Tabasco sauce

1-2 teaspoons Worcestershire sauce

4-5 tablespoons Pickapeppa sauce (available in most grocery stores)

4 ounces fontina cheese, thinly sliced

6 Po' Boy Rolls (page 22)

Heat half the olive oil in a large cast-iron skillet or on a griddle over medium heat and sauté the onions until caramelized. Remove and reserve. Season the beef slices with salt and pepper (not too much salt, though, because the various sauces and the cheese are somewhat salty).

Add the remaining oil to the skillet or griddle, increase the heat to medium-high, and brown the meat. Once the meat is browned, add the onions and Tabasco, Worcestershire, and Pickapeppa sauces, stir and heat thoroughly.

Separate the beef and onion mix into 6 roll-shaped portions right in the pan, and top with cheese. Press down each portion, folding some of the meat over the cheese to help melt the cheese.

Split the rolls, and butter and toast them. Assemble the sandwiches and cut them in half on the bias. Great with french fries to sop up all the juices.

Cobb Sandwich

Of all the sandwiches we serve at the Diner,
this is my favorite. It's a take-off on the famous Cobb salad that was originally
served at the Brown Derby in Hollywood. I guess you could call it
a salad in a bun. We used to serve it on po' boy rolls, but now we serve it on
rosemary focaccia rolls that we get from a local bakery.

SERVES 6

6	tablespoons mayonnaise (page 169)
2	tablespoons Dijon mustard
12	slices apple-smoked bacon or regular bacon (about 8 ounces)
6	rosemary focaccia rolls or Po' Boy Rolls (page 22)
1	pound smoked turkey, sliced paper-thin
6	slices tomato cut ¼ inch thick
2	avocados, peeled and sliced
2	cups finely shredded romaine or iceberg lettuce
6	tablespoons Bleu Cheese Dressing (page 108) or 6 tablespoons crumbled bleu cheese

Combine the mayonnaise and mustard in a small bowl, and set it aside. Griddle or pan-fry the bacon until crisp, and set this aside, too.

Split the rolls and toast them under the broiler. Spread the mustard-mayonnaise on the bottom half of each roll, then assemble the sandwiches in this order: 2 slices of bacon, a full layer of turkey slices, a slice of tomato, 3 or 4 slices of avocado, and lettuce. Spread bleu cheese dressing on the top halves of the buns or crumble a little bleu cheese over the lettuce and close up the sandwiches. Cut the sandwiches at an angle. Serve with chips or alone—it's really a meal in itself.

Pork Piccata Sandwich with Caper Vinaigrette

Piccata usually refers to the classic Italian dish that consists of veal scallops that are pounded thin, sautéed, and served with a sauce made with lemon juice and capers. This sandwich is a take-off on that idea, using breaded pork cutlets and a vinaigrette instead. You could do the same thing with chicken or turkey cutlets, too. These are juicy sandwiches, so have plenty of napkins handy.

SERVES 6

Vinaigrette:

1	shallot, peeled and minced
1	tablespoon minced parsley leaves
1	tablespoon small capers
3	tablespoons rice vinegar
9	tablespoons olive oil
	Kosher or sea salt
	Freshly ground white pepper

Breading:

½	cup flour
½	teaspoon kosher or sea salt
	Freshly ground white pepper
½	cup milk
1	egg
1	cup bread crumbs
2	tablespoons finely minced parsley
1	tablespoon minced fresh basil
¼	cup finely grated asiago cheese

1¾	pounds boneless pork loin, trimmed of fat and membrane
2	tablespoons unsalted butter
2	tablespoons olive oil
6	Hamburger Buns (page 22)
1½	cups shredded iceberg lettuce
12	paper-thin slices onion

To prepare the vinaigrette, whisk together the shallot, parsley, capers, and vinegar. Gradually whisk in the olive oil until thoroughly combined. Season with salt and pepper, and set aside.

Combine the flour, salt, and pepper in a bowl or on a large plate. In another bowl, whisk together the milk and egg to form an egg wash. In a third bowl, combine the bread crumbs, parsley, basil, and cheese.

Cut the pork into 12 slices each about ½ inch thick. Pound each slice of pork to a ¼-inch thickness. Dip the pork slices into the seasoned flour, then into the egg wash, and finally into the bread crumb mixture. Coat thoroughly. Heat the butter and olive oil in a sauté pan, and pan-fry the pork cutlets until golden brown on both sides.

Split the hamburger buns and toast them on the griddle or under the broiler. Assemble the sandwiches in this order: sprinkle a little lettuce on the bottom half of each bun, add 2 pork cutlets and 2 slices of onion. Drizzle 2 teaspoons of vinaigrette over all and close up the sandwich. This is good with fries and cole slaw.

Soft-Shell Crab Sandwich with Spicy Rémoulade

When soft-shell crabs are in season, this is the best sandwich of all.
You have to use fresh soft-shell crabs—they're just not the
same when they've been frozen—and always cook them the same day that you
buy them. You can pan-fry rather than deep-fry the crabs if
you like. If you cannot find soft-shell crabs, you can make a shrimp sandwich
instead, using the same breading and the rémoulade. If you
like, you can substitute Tartar Sauce (page 130) for the Spicy Rémoulade.

SERVES 6

6   soft-shell crabs

Breading:

1   egg
½   cup milk
½   cup flour
½   cup cornmeal
1   teaspoon salt
½-1   teaspoon freshly ground white
       pepper
1   teaspoon cayenne

       Peanut oil for deep-frying (or
       olive oil for pan-frying)
6   Hamburger Buns (page 22)
2   cups shredded iceberg lettuce
6   thin slices onion
       Spicy Rémoulade (recipe
       follows)
6   lemon wedges

Clean the crabs by lifting the top back on either side and removing the feathery gills and snipping off the eyes and beaks with scissors.

In a mixing bowl, whisk the egg and milk to form an egg wash. In another bowl, or on a large plate, combine the flour, cornmeal, salt, pepper, and cayenne. Dip the crabs into the flour mixture and shake off any excess. Then dip them into the egg wash, shake off the excess, and finally dip them back into the flour mixture. Coat thoroughly and again shake off any excess.

Deep-fry the crabs in 3 to 4 inches of peanut oil in a large cast-iron pan. Depending on the size of the crabs, they should take about 3 to 5 minutes to cook. Keep them warm in the oven as you finish them. To pan-fry the crabs, heat the olive oil in a large sauté pan and fry them, turning them once, until they're golden brown and crispy.

Split the buns, butter, and toast them. Make each sandwich with a little lettuce, a slice of onion, a crab, and about a tablespoon of Spicy Rémoulade. You can serve lemon wedges and additional rémoulade on the side.

Spicy Rémoulade

Great with any kind of seafood. Try it on grilled tuna or salmon sandwiches.

1   cup Sherry-Cayenne
     Mayonnaise (page 73)
1   tablespoon chopped scallions
2   tablespoons chopped celery
1   teaspoon chopped garlic
2   tablespoons chopped capers
1   tablespoon minced tarragon
2   tablespoons minced parsley
2   shakes Tabasco sauce

Combine all the ingredients and keep refrigerated until needed.

Reddened Snapper Sandwich with Guacamole

For a while, it was fashionable to serve blackened fish,
and it seemed like every restaurant had it on their menu. Just to be different,
we offered reddened fish in a sandwich. The achiote paste
gives the fish its color and also makes it a little spicy. You can buy achiote paste in
Latin American markets or make your own (page 134).
We use our local rock cod, which is often called Pacific snapper, and is
available year-round. Catfish is also good.
You can deep-fry or pan-fry the fish, whichever you prefer.

SERVES 6

Achiote Marinade:

Achiote Paste (page 134)
¼	cup fresh orange juice
¼	cup rice vinegar
½	teaspoon ground cumin seed
2	teaspoons oregano
	Pinch of kosher or sea salt
	Freshly ground black pepper to taste
2	garlic cloves, minced
1	tablespoon olive oil
6	fillets Pacific snapper or rock cod, 4½ ounces each

Breading:

½	cup flour
½	cup cornmeal
	Kosher or sea salt
	Freshly ground black pepper
1	cup buttermilk
	Peanut oil for deep-frying
6	Po' Boy Rolls or Hamburger Buns (page 22)

4	tablespoons mayonnaise (page 169)
2	cups shredded iceberg lettuce
½	red onion, cut into 6 paper-thin slices
1	lime
½	cup Guacamole (page 166)

To prepare the marinade, place the achiote paste, orange juice, vinegar, cumin, oregano, salt, and pepper in a blender and blend together. Add the garlic and oil and blend further until thoroughly emulsified. Dip the fish fillets in the marinade to coat, and marinate for at least 2 hours, or as long as overnight.

In a bowl or on a large plate, combine the flour and cornmeal, and season with salt and pepper. Put the buttermilk in a wide bowl. Dip the fillets in the buttermilk, shake off the excess; dip the fish in the breading, shaking off any excess coating. Fry the fillets in 3 to 4 inches of peanut oil in a cast-iron pan until golden brown, about 3 to 4 minutes.

Split the buns or rolls and toast them under the broiler. Lightly spread mayonnaise on the bottom half of each bun, and assemble the sandwiches in this order: a little lettuce, a slice of onion, a fish fillet, and a squeeze of lime juice. Spread 2 to 3 tablespoons of guacamole on the top half of each bun or roll, close up the sandwich, and cut it in half on the bias. This is good with Cole Slaw (page 162).

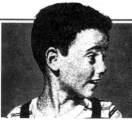

Grilled Eggplant Sandwich with Fontina and Watercress

We always offer one vegetarian sandwich on the menu,
and this has proven to be one of the most popular. It is made with eggplant
that has been marinated in an Asian-style sauce and then grilled.
(The marinade is also good for barbecued chicken or lamb.) You can use regular
eggplant or Japanese eggplant, but regular eggplant fits more
neatly on a round bun. For people who are on dairy-free diets, omit the fontina.

SERVES 6

Marinade:

¼	cup ketjap manis, or tamari soy sauce
½	cup olive oil
1-2	cloves minced garlic
1	tablespoon grated ginger
	Kosher or sea salt
	Freshly ground white pepper
1	regular eggplant cut into ½-inch slices, or 3-6 Japanese eggplants split lengthwise
6	slices red onion cut ¼ inch thick
6	thin slices fontina cheese
6	Hamburger Buns (page 22)
6	tablespoons Tomato Chutney (page 167)
3-4	tablespoons mayonnaise (page 169)
1	bunch watercress or cilantro

In a large mixing bowl, thoroughly combine the marinade ingredients. Brush the eggplant slices with the marinade and let marinate for 1 to 2 hours in a bowl or on a cookie sheet. If you are using Japanese eggplant, you can score the cut side of the eggplant so it will take in the marinade better, or cut it on the bias into ½-inch-thick slices, using several per sandwich.

Grill the onion and eggplant slices for about 2 minutes and turn. Top the eggplant with a slice of cheese, and grill 2 minutes more, or until onion and eggplant are tender and the cheese has melted. Stack the onion slices on top of the cheese.

Split the buns and toast them on the grill or under the broiler. Spread a tablespoon of Tomato Chutney on the bottom half of each roll and 2 teaspoons mayonnaise on the top half and assemble the sandwiches, putting a little watercress or cilantro in each one.

Italian Sausage Sandwich

You'll have to eat this sandwich with a knife and fork.
It's like a chili dog made with sausages and a tomato sauce.
We make it with hot Italian sausages, but if you don't like
spicy foods, get medium or mild sausages instead.

SERVES 6

Caramelized Onions:

1½-2 onions sliced top to bottom in thin wedges

1 tablespoon olive oil
Kosher or sea salt
Freshly ground pepper

Tomato Sauce:

3 tablespoons olive oil
4 cloves garlic, minced
1 tablespoon tomato paste
2 cups peeled and diced tomatoes
1 teaspoon red chile flakes
½ cup white or red wine
Kosher or sea salt
Freshly ground pepper
1 tablespoon minced basil

6 Italian sausages (about 1½ pounds), blanched
6 Hot Dog Buns or Po' Boy Rolls (page 22)
2 tablespoons unsalted butter
⅓ cup grated asiago cheese

Preheat oven to 375 to 400 degrees. Toss the onion slices and olive oil together with a little salt and pepper in an ovenproof casserole. Bake in the oven until golden brown, stirring occasionally, 20 to 30 minutes. Or you can slowly caramelize the onions in a cast-iron pan over medium heat on top of the stove, stirring occasionally.

To make the tomato sauce, heat 2 tablespoons of olive oil in a pan, add the garlic and tomato paste, and cook for 1 minute. Add the diced tomatoes and sauté 1 minute more. Then add the chile flakes, wine, salt, pepper, and basil, and cook over medium heat until the sauce thickens, about 10 to 15 minutes.

While the sauce is cooking, grill the sausages over a medium fire or heat them in a sauté pan over medium heat until browned and heated through. Split the rolls, spread 1 teaspoon butter on each, and toast on the grill or the griddle, or under the broiler. Place the sausages in the toasted buns and top with sauce, caramelized onions, and cheese. Serve it open-faced, with french fries or grilled potatoes on the side. For a great entrée, omit the rolls and serve the sausages with Polenta Cakes (page 160).

Diner Chili Dog

A good chili dog is another must for any diner. We make ours with Vienna Red Hots, the classic all-beef hot dog, but you can use any good-quality, old-fashioned hot dog (the kind with the skin on). You will need a batch of Sirloin and Black Bean Chili heated up and ready to dish out.

6   Vienna Red Hots
6   Hot Dog Buns (page 22)
3   cups Sirloin and Black Bean Chili (page 53)
1-1½ cups grated cheddar cheese
4   tablespoons minced red onion

Split the hot dogs and grill them over medium-high heat for 3 to 5 minutes. Split the buns and grill or toast them. Put the hot dogs on the buns, top with chili, and sprinkle with cheese and minced onions.

Bill Upson's Slaw Dog

Bill Upson claims that he grew up eating slaw dogs. He made us put this on the menu once, but it never sold. Now it's only made on special request—usually his.

6   hot dogs
6   Hot Dog Buns (page 22)
6   slices cheddar cheese
1   cup Cole Slaw (page 162)

Split the hot dogs and grill them over medium-high heat for 3 to 5 minutes. Split and grill or toast the buns. Put a hot dog on each bun, top it with a slice of cheese, and run it under the broiler just long enough to melt the cheese. Smother it with Cole Slaw. I'll have to admit—it seems like perfect beach food.

The Gil Dog

Gil Figueroa, one of our grill cooks, created this dog for Charles Toby, one of our sous-chefs. Like the Slaw Dog, this item is not on our menu. It's the kind of thing we throw together for ourselves when we realize it's 3:00 p.m. and we're starving to death. All the ingredients are always on hand, so it's nice and quick to fix.

Relish:

1   cup minced Bread and Butter Pickles (page 167)
½   red onion, finely minced
½   bunch cilantro, chopped
1   tomato, finely chopped

6   hot dogs
6   Hot Dog Buns (page 22)
12   slices fontina cheese

Combine the pickles, onion, cilantro, and tomato, and set it aside. Split the hot dogs and grill them over medium-high heat for 3 to 5 minutes. Split and grill or toast the buns. Put a hot dog on each bun, top it with two slices of cheese, and run it under the broiler just long enough to melt the cheese. Liberally sprinkle the relish down the entire length of the hot dog, enough to almost hide it. Open a beer and go sit outside where you can eat, drink, and enjoy.

SAL

CHAP

ADS

TER 5

SALADS
CHAPTER 5

To make great salads, you must use great ingredients—fresh greens, varied in texture and taste, fresh herbs, and the highest quality oils, vinegars, and mustards. I encourage people to grow as many of their salad vegetables as possible because homegrown greens and onions, radishes, tomatoes, cucumbers, and herbs can really make a world of difference. If you can't grow your own, try to find a market you can depend on for good produce.   You want everything to look as good as it tastes, so take care with the initial preparation of the salad ingredients. Use small-to medium-sized heads of lettuce so the leaves can be left whole, or only torn once. Consider the ease of eating when cutting up the other ingredients. If the recipe calls for cooked vegetables, be careful not to overcook them.   Greens should be carefully separated, washed, and dried. Use a salad spinner to dry them quickly without damaging them. I was taught to wrap them gently in a towel and spin them around over my head outside—quite a trick in a Minnesota winter!   In making vinaigrette dressings, I use a ratio of three parts oil to one part vinegar. For a milder flavor, you can use four to one. Extra-virgin olive oil has such a strong flavor that in most vinaigrette dressings to be used on greens, I use it in small amounts, about one part extra-virgin to two to three parts of the lighter "pure" olive oil.   You can prepare all the elements for a salad ahead of time, including the dressing, then put it all together just before you're ready to serve it. Prepped ahead, it only takes a moment. Greens should always be dressed lightly and served "face up" so that they look and taste their best. The best way to toss a salad is to do it gently with your hands. Then you can be sure the greens are nicely coated but not drowning in dressing.   Nowadays there are so many different kinds of wonderful salad greens available, it's fun to shop around for the more unusual varieties. Try experimenting also with watercress, kale, and Chinese and Japanese greens. Use combinations with different colors, textures, and flavors. We try to keep our salads interesting by using at least two or three different kinds of greens in each one. Each salad also has its own special dressing, too, but again, you should feel free to experiment.

At the time we opened Fog City Diner, everyone was using all these new, somewhat esoteric greens in their salads instead of iceberg lettuce. We used all the same esoteric greens, but we just didn't talk about which field they came from, on which farm, or what time of day they were harvested. In fact, we didn't even name them. That's why we decided to call our house salad "Unintimidating Mixed Greens." We offer the salad with either the house vinaigrette or with a bleu cheese dressing. When I fix it for myself, I use the vinaigrette dressing, and garnish the salad with crumbled bleu cheese—best of both worlds.

We use many different kinds of greens at the Diner. Some of them are very common, and you can get these at your local supermarket; some of the more unusual ones you might find at specialty markets or farmers' markets. We choose from these varieties, depending on the season and what's available at the time: red and green butter lettuce, red and green romaine, red oak leaf lettuce, Cybele Batarian, green oak leaf lettuce, Lollo Rosso, Salad Bowl lettuce, Biondo, endive, Brune d'Hiver, chicory frisée, arugula, Napa cabbage, Bloomsdale spinach, escarole.

Many grocery stores are now selling prewashed mixed greens, ready to use. They are a little expensive, but there's no waste, and they save on preparation time. Be on the safe side, though, and give them a rinse and a spin.

SERVES 6

1½-2 cups mixed greens per person
¾ cup House Vinaigrette Dressing or Bleu Cheese Dressing (page 108)
½ cup loosely packed herbs, optional (basil, cilantro, tarragon, or chervil)
Freshly ground black pepper

Thoroughly wash and dry the greens, and keep refrigerated in a towel or salad spinner until ready to serve. Just before serving, toss the greens with one of the dressings in a large bowl. If you like, you can add one or two of the herbs to give a little more flavor to the greens. We just pick the leaves from the stems. If the basil leaves are really large, you can tear them. Pass the pepper mill around after the salads have been served.

House Vinaigrette

This dressing will keep for several days in the refrigerator. It can also be used with the Tahini Chicken Salad (page 119) and the Mushroom Salad (page 114).

2 tablespoons balsamic vinegar
2 tablespoons sherry vinegar
2 shallots, peeled and minced
2 teaspoons Dijon mustard
 Kosher or sea salt
 Freshly ground white pepper to taste
½ cup olive oil
¼ cup virgin olive oil

In a mixing bowl, combine the vinegars, shallots, mustard, salt, and pepper. Gradually whisk in the oils and continue to whisk until thoroughly emulsified. Keep refrigerated. Mix the dressing well again just before using, as the ingredients will separate.

Bleu Cheese Dressing

This dressing can also be used with Waldorf salads and with burgers. Use a good-flavored cheese such as Maytag, Roquefort, Stilton, Gorgonzola, or Danish bleu.

3 ounces Roquefort cheese
1 cup mayonnaise (page 169)
3 tablespoons sour cream
2 teaspoons fresh lemon juice
 Kosher or sea salt
 Freshly ground white pepper to taste
1-2 drops Worcestershire sauce
1-2 drops Tabasco sauce
¼ cup finely minced celery, including leaves
2 scallions, minced
1 tablespoon minced chives

Break up the cheese into small pieces and reserve. In a mixing bowl, combine the mayonnaise, sour cream, lemon juice, salt, pepper, Worcestershire sauce, and Tabasco sauce and whisk well. Gently stir in the cheese, celery, scallions and chives. Do not overmix, as the cheese will turn an unappetizing blue-grey. Keep refrigerated.

Caesar Salad

Caesar salad is probably the most popular salad of all
at any restaurant, and the Diner is no exception. In fact, we serve about
2,000 Caesar salads every month! Altogether you need 1 cup
of shredded cheese. When you shred the cheese, use the small circular-shaped
hole grater rather than the star-shaped surface that makes
it crumble. You can cut the lettuce up or leave it whole—it's up to you. We use whole
leaves at Mustards and Buckeye, but cut them at
the Diner. When you make the special croutons for this salad, you might as well
make plenty. They're addictive! Anchovies are a critical
ingredient in a Caesar salad, so be sure you use good quality anchovies.

SERVES 6

Caesar Salad Croutons:

½	loaf sourdough bread or baguette
¼	cup olive oil or melted butter
3	cloves garlic, mashed
	Freshly ground pepper

Caesar Dressing:

8-10	anchovy fillets
2	cloves garlic
3	tablespoons red wine vinegar
1	scant tablespoon Dijon mustard
¼	cup shredded parmesan or asiago cheese
1	teaspoon Worcestershire sauce
1	egg
¾	cup olive oil
4	heads romaine lettuce, inner leaves only
¾	cup finely shredded parmesan or asiago cheese

Preheat oven to 325 degrees. To prepare the croutons, cut off the crust and tear the bread into small, irregular pieces. Combine the oil, garlic, and pepper in a bowl. Toss the croutons with the oil mixture and place them in an even layer on a cookie sheet. Bake for 5 to 10 minutes, until the croutons are golden brown and crisp all the way through. Remove them from the oven and allow to cool.

To prepare the dressing in a blender, mince 2 anchovies and set them aside. Place the remaining anchovies, garlic, vinegar, mustard, ¼ cup cheese, Worcestershire sauce, and egg in the blender, and blend until smooth. With the blender running, add the oil in a steady stream and continue to blend until emulsified. (If you don't have a blender, mince the garlic and the anchovies, and set aside a few tablespoons of the minced anchovies. Combine the rest of the anchovies in a small bowl with the garlic, vinegar, mustard, cheese, and Worcestershire sauce. Break the egg into another bowl, and beat the garlic-vinegar mixture into the egg. Gradually whisk in the oil and continue to whisk until emulsified.) Stir in the reserved minced anchovies.

Separate the romaine leaves; wash and dry them, and tear them into pieces. Place the lettuce in a large salad bowl and toss with the dressing, croutons, and ½ cup of the grated cheese. (If you don't have a big enough salad bowl, make the salad in two batches.) Just before serving, sprinkle each serving with some of the remaining cheese.

Asparagus and Crottin Cheese Salad

Laura Chenel in Santa Rosa, California, produces an excellent Crottin cheese, a French-inspired cheese made from goats' milk. In the aging process, the cheese develops an edible crust, so it's vaguely like a camembert or brie. Once aged, the cheese is packed in an herbed olive oil. It's especially delicious with asparagus or artichokes. If you can't get it, use another kind of goat cheese. This is a real quick salad to make.

SERVES 6

6	ounces Crottin cheese
2	pounds asparagus
½	head escarole, blanched white leaves only
1	head frisée, trimmed of dark green outer leaves
1	bunch arugula
1	tablespoon minced shallots
3	tablespoons balsamic vinegar
	Pinch of kosher or sea salt
	Big pinch freshly ground black pepper
½	cup extra-virgin olive oil
3	tablespoons sliced shallots
3-4	tablespoons sliced toasted almonds

Crumble the cheese and set it aside to come to room temperature. Snap off and discard the tough ends of the asparagus. Peel the asparagus if you wish, and cut it on the bias into 2-inch pieces. Blanch the asparagus in boiling salted water for 1 or 2 minutes. Drain and chill.

Wash the escarole, frisée, and arugula and spin dry. Keep cold until ready to use. To prepare the dressing, combine the minced shallots, balsamic vinegar, salt, and pepper. When the salt is dissolved, whisk in the oil.

Just before serving, dress the greens with part of the dressing and arrange them on the plates. Dress the asparagus with the remaining dressing and arrange them around the greens. Liberally sprinkle sliced shallots, nuts, and crumbled cheese over each salad.

Summer Tomato Salad

Believe me, this salad is good only with vine-ripened tomatoes—
preferably from your own garden. Life is too short to bother with tasteless tomatoes.
I like to use a combination of red and yellow tomatoes to make
the salad more colorful, but if yellow tomatoes are unavailable, substitute with additional
red tomatoes, whatever is best. Sometimes you can find
unusual varieties at farmers' markets—like the Green Grape, which looks just
like a huge grape, or the Green Zebra, which has light and dark
green stripes. The herbs can be chopped or hand torn rather than minced, if you prefer.
Grilled or toasted bread rubbed with garlic would make
a delicious accompaniment.

SERVES 6 TO 8

Vinaigrette:

2	tablespoons rice vinegar
1	tablespoon Dijon mustard
1	tablespoon minced shallots
	Pinch of kosher or sea salt
1	teaspoon freshly ground black pepper
4	tablespoons light olive oil
2	tablespoons extra-virgin olive oil
3-4	red vine-ripened tomatoes (12-18 slices)
5-6	yellow vine-ripened tomatoes (12-18 slices)
1-2	dozen red cherry tomatoes (2-4 per salad)
1-2	dozen yellow pear tomatoes (2-4 per salad)
5	tablespoons minced chervil leaves
2	tablespoons minced chives
1	tablespoon chiffonade of mint

To prepare the vinaigrette, place the vinegar, mustard, shallots, salt, and pepper in a mixing bowl and combine. Gradually whisk in the oils and continue to whisk until thoroughly emulsified.

Cut the tomatoes into ⅜-inch-thick slices. Arrange on serving plates, alternating the red and yellow tomato slices. Toss the cherry and pear tomatoes in a portion of the vinaigrette. Drizzle the remaining vinaigrette on the sliced tomatoes and arrange the cherry and pear tomatoes on the plate. Combine the chervil, chives, and mint and sprinkle some over each salad.

Mushroom Salad with Fennel and Seasoned Pecans

When summer is over, and we can no longer get good vine-ripened tomatoes,
we serve this salad instead. We use a combination of
shiitakes and whatever edible wild mushrooms are available at the time.
The trimmed green of the chicory can be added to soups or
sautéed with vegetables. Try the Sherry Vinaigrette on a mixed
green salad with goat cheese and toasted pecans.

Serves 6

1	head Belgian endive
1	bunch arugula (about 8 ounces), or watercress, coarse stems removed
1	head chicory frisée, trimmed of green part, or 1 head escarole, white inner leaves only
1	head butter lettuce or ½ head romaine lettuce, inner leaves only

Sherry Vinaigrette:

3	tablespoons sherry vinegar
2	teaspoons Dijon mustard
2	shallots, peeled and minced
	Kosher or sea salt
	Freshly ground pepper
3	tablespoons extra-virgin olive oil
6	tablespoons light olive oil

Marinade:

2	scallions, minced
2	teaspoons tamari soy sauce
3	tablespoons Sherry Vinaigrette
2	teaspoons sesame oil

1	fennel bulb
4-6	shiitake mushrooms, stemmed and cleaned
4-6	chanterelle mushrooms or morels or hedgehogs
3-4	tablespoons olive oil
	Kosher or sea salt
	Freshly ground pepper
2	cups seasoned pecan halves (page 228)

Thoroughly wash and dry the greens, and lightly toss them together in a large mixing bowl. Keep refrigerated.

To prepare the Sherry Vinaigrette, mix together the sherry vinegar, mustard, shallots, salt, and pepper in a small mixing bowl. Whisk in both olive oils until emulsified. Set aside.

Whisk together the marinade ingredients. Slice the fennel very thinly across from the top to the bottom (we use a Japanese or a French mandoline to do this), combine it with a little of the marinade, and set aside.

If the mushrooms are small, they can be left whole; if they're really large, cut them in half. Lightly toss them in olive oil, and season with salt and pepper to taste. Roast them in a preheated 350-degree oven until tender and caramelized, but not mushy. (If you prefer, you can sauté the mushrooms in a hot nonstick skillet with no additional oil.) Pour just enough marinade over the mushrooms to lightly coat, and then toss well. Set aside to marinate for about an hour.

When you are ready to serve, toss the greens with the Sherry Vinaigarette and place on serving plates. Top with the marinated fennel and mushrooms, and garnish with the pecan halves.

Artichoke, Spinach, Olive and Endive Salad

There's a special kind of spinach that I like to use in this salad:
it has a small, crisp, crinkly leaf that supports the weight of the artichokes well.
It is most commonly called Bloomsdale, but may go by other names.
If you can't find Bloomsdale, any spinach will work. You can use any size artichokes,
but the large ones will give you better-looking slices of heart.

3 large artichokes or
10 small ones
1 lemon
1 tablespoon flour
1-2 bay leaves
1 teaspoon salt
1 teaspoon whole black
peppercorns
1 cup diced tomato
1 cup white wine

Lemon Vinaigrette:

3 tablespoons fresh lemon juice
1 tablespoon Dijon mustard
1 tablespoon minced shallots
Kosher or sea salt
Freshly ground pepper
6 tablespoons light olive oil
3 tablespoons extra-virgin olive oil

2 bunches arugula
3 cups spinach (Bloomsdale, preferably), coarse stems removed
2 heads endive or frisée
½ cup pitted Kalamata (Greek) olives, cut into wedges
⅓-½ cup Green Goddess Dressing (recipe follows) or ½ cup crumbled goat cheese or feta cheese

To prepare the artichokes, trim off the stems flush with the base and cut off the top third of the artichoke. Snap off the outer leaves down to the heart. Cut the lemon in half, and rub it all over the exposed surfaces. Place the artichokes in a pot with the flour, bay leaves, salt, peppercorns, tomato, and wine. Add enough water to cover, and simmer until tender. Drain and cool. When cool enough to handle, gently clean out the choke and cut the hearts into wedges or slices.

To prepare the vinaigrette, combine the lemon juice, mustard, shallots, and salt and pepper in a mixing bowl. Gradually whisk in the oils until thoroughly emulsified. Toss the artichoke hearts with enough vinaigrette to coat thoroughly. Marinate at least 2 hours (overnight is OK).

Thoroughly wash and dry the arugula, spinach, and endive, and combine in a large mixing bowl. Lightly toss the greens with the remaining vinaigrette and transfer to serving plates. Place the marinated artichoke hearts and

olives on top of the greens. Drizzle each portion with some of the Green Goddess Dressing, or sprinkle with goat or feta cheese.

Green Goddess Dressing

This dressing is also nice on Bibb or butter lettuce, as there are a lot of flavors in the dressing to brighten up the greens. You might want to thin it a bit with ice water or lemon juice.

½ cup mayonnaise (page 169)
1 anchovy, chopped
2½ tablespoons chopped Italian parsley
1 tablespoon chopped chives
1 tablespoon tarragon vinegar
3 tablespoons minced tarragon
1 scallion, minced

In a blender or processor, blend together the mayonnaise, anchovy, parsley, chives, and vinegar. Remove from blender and stir in the tarragon and scallions. You could also mince all the herbs and anchovies and combine them with the mayonnaise with a spoon. Keep refrigerated.

Crab Louis with Thousand Island Dressing

A crab Louis will only be successful if you use fresh sweet crabmeat,
so don't try to make this with canned or frozen stuff. Use your
favorite vinaigrette to dress the greens. We use the House Vinaigrette,
but the Sherry Vinaigrette (page 114) would also be good.
The crab itself is dressed with a traditional Thousand Island Dressing.

SERVES 6

9   cups mixed greens
6   tablespoons House Vinaigrette (page 108)
1   pound crabmeat, cleaned of any shell fragments
18 cherry tomatoes or wedges of ripe tomato
6   hard-boiled eggs, cut in wedges
6   wedges or 12 slices avocado (optional)
6   lemon wedges
2   cups Thousand Island Dressing (recipe follows)
2   tablespoons chopped and squeezed parsley

Lightly toss the greens in the vinaigrette and divide them among the plates. Place a mound of crabmeat on top of the greens and surround it with the tomatoes and wedges of hard-boiled egg, avocado, and lemon. Dress each serving with 2 tablespoons of the Thousand Island Dressing and garnish with parsley. Serve with the remaining dressing on the side.

Thousand Island Dressing

This is the classic sauce for crab or shrimp Louis. It is also good on the Soft-shell Crab Sandwiches (page 94).

1¼ cups mayonnaise (page 169)
¼   cup Heinz ketchup
1   tablespoon cognac
3   drops Tabasco sauce
2   tablespoons minced red onion
3   scallions, minced
¼   cup minced Bread and Butter Pickles (page 167)
    Kosher or sea salt
    Freshly ground pepper

In a mixing bowl, combine all the ingredients and mix thoroughly. Keep refrigerated.

Cold Rare Sirloin with Tapenade, Onions, and Watercress

For this salad, you need very, very thin, evenly cut slices of rare beef.
At the Diner, we grill the meat ourselves and use a
meat slicer to cut it. For convenience's sake, you can buy thinly sliced rare
roast beef from a deli, or use leftover roast beef cut thin.
Marinating the onions in lemon juice will turn them a bright pink.
It will also soften them up a bit.

SERVES 6

1	red onion, cut into 12 paper-thin slices
	Juice of 1 lemon
1	tablespoon champagne vinegar
2	tablespoons Dijon mustard
4	tablespoons olive oil
⅓	cup Tapenade (recipe follows)
	Olive oil to thin Tapenade
6-8	leaves minced basil and/or Italian parsley
18	paper-thin slices of rare roasted beef sirloin
12	sprigs watercress
1	tablespoon minced scallions
1	tablespoon julienned basil
	Cracked black pepper

Place the slices of red onion in a mixing bowl with the lemon juice, and let it marinate for 30 minutes. Meanwhile, prepare a dressing by combining the vinegar and mustard in a mixing bowl and gradually whisking in the olive oil. Continue to whisk until thoroughly emulsified. Put the tapenade in a third bowl, and stir in enough olive oil to make it of a spreadable consistency. Add the basil or parsley and mix.

When you're ready to serve, spread about 1 teaspoon of the tapenade on each serving plate, lay 3 slices of sirloin over the tapenade, and drizzle on a tablespoon or so of the dressing. Spread a few of the onion rings on top of the meat. Dress the watercress with the dressing and place on top of the sirloin, too. Garnish with the minced scallions, julienned basil, and cracked black pepper.

Tapenade

Tapenade is an olive paste that orginially came from southern France. It makes a great appetizer spread on croutons or hard-boiled eggs. It also makes a good dip for raw vegetables. You can buy tapenade in jars (it will either be labeled as tapenade or olive paste) but this is one of those things that tastes so much better homemade. Use the best olives and anchovies available.

1½	cups black Greek or Niçoise olives, pitted and rinsed
2	anchovy fillets, rinsed
1½	tablespoons small capers
1	clove garlic, smashed
	Juice of 1 lemon
¼	cup olive oil
	Freshly ground pepper
2	tablespoons chopped basil

Using either a mortar and pestle or a processor, combine the black olives, anchovy fillets, capers, garlic, lemon juice, olive oil, and pepper. Mix thoroughly. If the mixture appears too thick, add a bit more olive oil. Pour into a small bowl and stir in the basil. Store leftovers in a glass jar, float a little olive oil on top, and it will keep refrigerated for months.

BBQ Pork Salad with Creamy BBQ Dressing

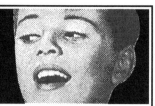

My partners "Boo" and "Up" once returned from a trip to the East Coast talking about a barbecued pork salad they had eaten. It's hard to duplicate a dish you've never seen, or tasted, or had the idea for in the first place, but I tried, and this is what I came up with based on their descriptions. A couple of years later I ate at the restaurant they had been to and sampled the original. Believe me, that salad and mine are not at all alike.

SERVES 6

2 pork tenderloins, about
   1½ pounds in all
4 tablespoons BBQ Pork Spice
   Blend (page 226)

Lime Vinaigrette:
Juice of 2 limes
1 tablespoon minced shallots
⅓ cup olive oil
   Kosher or sea salt
   Freshly ground pepper

½ head shredded Napa cabbage
   or your choice of crisp greens
2 cups julienned jicama
   Creamy BBQ Dressing (recipe
   follows)
2 tablespoons chopped chives

Remove any fat and sinew from the pork tenderloins and rub each with 2 tablespoons of the spice blend. Grill the pork until it reaches an internal temperature of 139 degrees. Let the meat rest for 15 minutes and cut it on the bias into 18 slices.

Whisk together the lime juice, shallots, olive oil, salt, and pepper. and toss it with the shredded cabbage and julienned jicama. Divide this evenly among the plates and top each with 3 slices of pork. Drizzle Creamy BBQ Dressing over the pork, and garnish each salad with chopped chives.

Creamy BBQ Dressing
Any leftover dressing may be used for crab, shrimp, or pork sandwiches.

1 tablespoon olive oil
3 tablespoons BBQ Pork Spice
   Blend (page 226)
⅓ cup mayonnaise (page 169)
⅓ cup sour cream
¼ cup buttermilk

Combine the oil and spice blend in a sauté pan and heat it until it becomes aromatic. Cool it slightly, and stir in the mayonnaise, sour cream, and buttermilk. Store in the refrigerator.

Tahini Chicken Salad

The Thai basil used in this recipe is a variegated purple-reddish-green in color, and is available in Asian markets and specialty stores as are all the other Asian ingredients called for. (You can get seeds for this variety if you're interested in growing your own.) If you can't get Thai basil, a combination of purple basil and green basil will give a similar effect. We poach the chicken on the bone to keep it moist and more flavorful. After you remove the meat from the bones, the poaching liquid can be cooked further with the bones to make a nice broth.

SERVES 6

3   whole chicken breasts

Poaching Broth:

3   tablespoons rice vinegar
3   tablespoons white wine
1   tablespoon dark soy sauce
1   1-inch piece of ginger, peeled and thinly sliced
1   3-inch piece of lemon grass, thinly sliced
2   star anise
1   teaspoon cracked peppercorns
2   teaspoons coriander seeds, crushed
1   bay leaf

Tahini Dressing:

¼   cup tahini
¼   cup coconut milk
½   minced jalapeño chile, seeded
2   teaspoons brown sugar
2   tablespoons rice vinegar
2   tablespoons olive oil
2   tablespoons double black soy sauce or tamari soy sauce
1   teaspoon minced garlic
1½   teaspoons peeled and grated ginger

4   cups mixed greens
2   cups shredded red cabbage and endive
1   cucumber, peeled, seeded, and sliced into half moons
2   teaspoons julienned Thai basil leaves
2   tablespoons cilantro leaves
12-16   red cherry tomatoes
6-8   tablespoons House Vinaigrette (page 108)

Place the chicken breasts in a large saucepan and add the poaching broth ingredients. Bring to a strong boil, lower the heat, and simmer for 15 minutes. Check to see if the chicken is cooked through to the bone. If not, return to simmer 10 to 15 additional minutes as needed. Remove the pan from heat, and let stand for 30 minutes. Remove the chicken and allow it to cool. Bone and skin the breasts; cut the meat into thin slices and reserve.

To prepare the tahini dressing, place all the ingredients in a blender and blend until thoroughly emulsified.

Combine the salad greens, cucumber, basil, cilantro, and cherry tomatoes in a mixing bowl. Dress lightly with House Vinaigrette, and transfer to serving plates, mounding the salad in the center. Place chicken slices on top of the greens, and drizzle the chicken with about 2 tablespoons tahini dressing per plate.

LARGE

CHAP

PLATES

LARGE PLATES

CHAPTER 6

Well since we called the appetizers "small plates" on the menu, it only made sense to follow suit and call the entrées "large plates," and that's what we did. Our large plates are dishes that would be considered standard diner fare, except that we put our own twist on them—a little curry in the chicken pot pie, barbecue sauce in the braised short ribs, succotash over rabbit. It's not exactly what your local diner had.   Partly because we're within a stone's throw of the Bay, and partly because people are so concerned about health and weight these days, we serve a ton of seafood. Each day we run two fish specials that are not on the printed menu, one that is off the grill, which is the easiest way to adapt for people with special diets, and another that is sautéed or griddled.   Many of our other large plates come off the grill, too. If you don't have the energy to fire up your barbecue and your home kitchen doesn't have a "grill station," you can broil, sauté, or pan-sear any of the grilled dishes. They will taste different but will still be good. For information on grilling and on cooking fish, see page 229.   Try to use only the freshest meat, poultry, and fish. The texture and flavor of the finished food will be so much better if you do. Different fish can be substituted in the recipes, if the texture and density of the flesh is similar. For example, you can use swordfish for the tuna or mahimahi, and halibut for the salmon. Trout and Petrale sole are easier to grill bone-in and skin-on versus filleted.   The vegetable side dishes that come with the large plates can be interchanged according to your personal preference. Always take seasonal availability into consideration, too.

Grilled Salmon with Peas and Asparagus

Salmon is so much fun to cook because its flavor combines well
with many different vegetables and sauces.
I think this is the best way to serve the first spring salmon of the year.
It's good with Steamed New Potatoes (page 159).

SERVES 6

6   salmon fillets, about 7 ounces
     each

Aioli:

2   egg yolks
4   cloves garlic, peeled and minced
     Juice of 2 lemons, or 2
     tablespoons champagne or
     rice vinegar
1¾-2 cups olive oil
     Kosher or sea salt
     Freshly ground pepper

Vegetables:

¾   cup water
2   cups fresh young peas or sugar
     snap peas
18   asparagus spears, cut on the bias
     into 1½-inch-long pieces
1   tablespoon minced shallots or
     scallions
     Kosher or sea salt
     Freshly ground pepper to taste
1   tablespoon chiffonade of mint
1   tablespoon unsalted butter or
     extra-virgin olive oil

     Olive oil
     Kosher or sea salt
     Freshly ground pepper to taste
     Steamed New Potatoes
     (page 159), optional

To prepare the aioli, using a blender, processor, or whisk, add the lemon juice or vinegar and garlic to the egg yolks, whisking until the yolks are thick and light lemon colored. Slowly add the olive oil, whisking until the mixture is emulsified. Season with salt and pepper.

To prepare the vegetables, place the water in a large skillet or sauté pan and bring to a boil. Add the peas, asparagus, and shallots or scallions. Cook over medium heat until the water has almost evaporated, and season to taste with salt and pepper. Add the mint and the butter or oil, and cook to a glaze.

Lightly brush the salmon fillets with olive oil and season with salt and pepper. Grill over a medium fire, 2 minutes a side.

Serve with the aioli on top of the salmon and the vegetables surrounding the fish.

Grilling adds a smokiness that works well with this light-flavored fish.
The pearl onions retain some of their crispness while
the artichokes become tender. Lots of chopped parsley finishes this dish.
If you can get Italian cipollini onions, substitute them for the pearl
onions. You can use mahimahi instead of tuna. For a simpler dish, you can
just serve the grilled fish with Tomato Vinaigrette (recipe follows).

SERVES 6

6 tuna fillets, 7 ounces each

Vinaigrette:

2 shallots, minced
3 tablespoons rice or champagne vinegar
1 tablespoon Dijon mustard
   Kosher or sea salt
   Freshly ground pepper
½ cup olive oil
½ cup chopped parsley or basil or a mixture of the two

2 tablespoons olive oil
1 tablespoon shallots, minced
1 teaspoon thyme
24 pearl onions, peeled and cut in half
⅓ cup white wine
4 large or 12 small artichokes, cooked (page 115)

   Olive oil
   Kosher or sea salt
   Freshly ground pepper to taste
1 lemon, cut in wedges
3 tablespoons chopped parsley

   Tomato Vinaigrette, optional (recipe follows)

Combine the vinaigrette ingredients except the olive oil. Whisk in the oil until emulsified.

Combine the olive oil, shallots, thyme, and pearl onions in a sauté pan, and cook over medium heat for 2 minutes or until lightly browned. Add the white wine and braise for 5 minutes, or until the onions are cooked through. Quarter the artichoke hearts and add to the onions. Sauté until the artichokes are heated through, tossing occasionally to mix.

Lightly brush the tuna with olive oil and season with salt and pepper. Grill over a medium fire, 2 to 3 minutes a side.

Place the onion and artichoke stew on a platter and the fish on top. Drizzle the vinaigrette on the fish and garnish with the lemon wedges and lots of chopped parsley.

Tomato Vinaigrette

Definitely only good made with summer tomatoes, this is like a *salade Niçoise* without the eggs, potatoes, beans, and lettuce. Serve it with grilled meat or poultry, or with any other grilled fish.

3 tomatoes, peeled, seeded, and diced or 2 baskets cherry tomatoes cut in half
½ cup Niçoise or Kalamata olives, pitted
3 tablespoons minced shallots
3 tablespoons capers
2 tablespoons chiffonade of basil
1 tablespoon minced chives or scallions
1 teaspoon salt
½ teaspoon freshly ground black pepper
¼ cup red wine vinegar
¾ cup olive oil

Combine the tomatoes, olives, shallots, capers, basil, chives, salt, and pepper and reserve. Shortly before serving, whisk together the vinegar and olive oil and pour it over the tomatoes and olives. Gently stir together.

Pan-Seared Mahimahi with Sautéed Spinach and Caramelized Shallots

This will also work well with spearfish, trout, or sea scallops. You can substitute Jalapeño Mint Butter for the vinaigrette if you prefer (recipe follows).

SERVES 6

½ pound shallots, peeled and sliced into thin rings
1 tablespoon olive oil
Kosher or sea salt
Freshly ground white pepper

Vinaigrette:
1 tablespoon red wine vinegar
2 tablespoons Dijon mustard
1 tablespoon minced fresh tarragon
¼ cup olive oil

3 tablespoons olive oil
6 mahimahi fillets, about 7 ounces each

Sautéed Spinach:
2-3 tablespoons olive oil
1 tablespoon minced garlic
2½-3 pounds spinach leaves, washed and dried
Kosher or sea salt
Freshly ground white pepper

Jalapeño Mint Butter, optional (recipe follows)

Preheat the oven to 375 degrees. On a baking sheet, mix together the shallots, oil, salt, and pepper, thoroughly coating the shallots. Bake in the oven for 15 to 25 minutes, stirring occasionally, until caramelized and crispy.

For the vinaigrette, mix together the vinegar, Dijon mustard, and tarragon. Whisk in the olive oil and set aside.

Heat the olive oil on a griddle, or in a cast-iron skillet or a non-stick pan over medium heat. Cook the mahimahi until golden brown, about 2 minutes on each side. Place in the oven on low heat (200 degrees) while you prepare the spinach.

Heat 2 tablespoons olive oil in a separate sauté pan and cook the garlic for 1 minute over medium heat. Add the spinach and stir until just wilted. Season with salt and pepper.

Place the fish on a serving plate, drizzle with the vinaigrette and sprinkle liberally with the caramelized shallots. Serve with the spinach and any remaining vinaigrette on the side.

Jalapeño Mint Butter
Prepare this just before serving the fish, as it should be just melted and frothy. It is also great with steamed crab or lobster.

3 tablespoons minced fresh mint leaves
2 jalapeños roasted, seeded, and minced
2 scallions, minced
1 cup butter
Kosher or sea salt to taste

Combine the mint, jalapeños, and scallions and reserve. Just before serving, quickly melt the butter until foaming, add the reserved ingredients, and salt to taste. Pour over the cooked fish in place of the vinaigrette.

Grilled Halibut with Beet-Horseradish Rémoulade

I love beets and horseradish and am always surprised how many converts to those two vegetables this sauce makes. The beets can be cooked the day before, if desired. Sautéed Spinach (see preceding recipe) and Steamed New Potatoes (page 159) would make good side dishes.

SERVES 6

6   halibut fillets, about 7 ounces each

Beet-Horseradish Rémoulade:

2   bunches small golden or red beets, 1½ to 2 cups
1   tablespoon stone-ground mustard
3   tablespoons rice or champagne vinegar
½   cup olive oil
2   tablespoons minced shallots
1   tablespoon chopped chives
¼   teaspoon kosher or sea salt
⅛   teaspoon freshly ground pepper
1   tablespoon freshly grated horseradish

Olive oil
Kosher or sea salt
Freshly ground pepper
1   lemon, cut in wedges
Sautéed Spinach (page 128), optional
Steamed New Potatoes (page 159), optional

Bake the beets at 350 degrees or boil them until fork tender. Allow them to cool, then slip off the skins, and grate the beets. Combine the mustard, vinegar, ½ cup olive oil, shallots, chives, ¼ teaspoon salt, and ⅛ teaspoon pepper and mix thoroughly. Toss with the beets and grated horseradish. Reserve.

Lightly brush the halibut fillets with olive oil and season with salt and pepper. Grill over medium heat, 2 to 3 minutes a side.

Place halibut fillets on a platter and top with the beet rémoulade. Garnish with lemon wedges. Serve with Sautéed Spinach and Steamed New Potatoes if desired.

Petrale Sole with Tartar Sauce

We use the local Petrale sole, which is a delicate, sweet-flavored fish.
If you can't get it, use any type of sole or flounder or other flatfish. For best results,
use several skillets for cooking so the fish is not overcrowded.
This dish is good with buttered green beans and Steamed New Potatoes (page 159).

SERVES 6

6	fillets Petrale sole, 6 ounces each
½	cup flour
1	teaspoon kosher or sea salt
½	teaspoon freshly ground pepper
3	tablespoons butter
2	tablespoons chopped parsley
	Tartar Sauce (recipe follows)
	Lemon wedges

Sift the flour, salt, and pepper onto a large plate and dredge the sole in the mixture, shaking off any excess flour. Heat 1 tablespoon of butter over medium heat in a large skillet, sauté pan, or on a griddle. When hot and foaming, add a sole fillet and cook for 1 to 1½ minutes per side, until golden brown. Be careful not to overcook this delicate fish. Place on a serving platter and keep warm in the oven while cooking the remaining fish.

Sprinkle with chopped parsley. Serve with a large dollop of Tartar Sauce and plenty of lemon wedges.

Tartar Sauce
This is good with any fried fish. It's especially good on Soft-shell Crab Sandwiches (page 94).

1	cup mayonnaise (page 169)
2	tablespoons minced gherkins
2	teaspoons minced onion
2	teaspoons minced celery leaves
2	teaspoons minced parsley
2	teaspoons minced chives
1	tablespoon lemon juice
1	tablespoon capers
2	teaspoons caper juice
⅛	teaspoon kosher or sea salt
⅛	teaspoon freshly ground white pepper
1	teaspoon cayenne

Combine all the tartar sauce ingredients and set aside in the refrigerator.

This is a hearty fish dish. The mushrooms are cooked up
in the gingery scallion butter which becomes the sauce. You can use any
kind of fresh mushrooms for the sauce, or try a combination
of fresh and dried mushrooms (about 1 cup dried plus 3 cups fresh). Soak the
dried mushrooms in warm water to rehydrate them, and save
the water for the sauce. We serve this with Roasted Potatoes (page 159).

SERVES 6

6	swordfish steaks, about 7 ounces each
	Olive oil
	Kosher or sea salt
	Freshly ground pepper
6	tablespoons butter
1	tablespoon minced shallot
5	cups sliced fresh mushrooms
¾	cup white wine (or Vegetable Stock, page 224, or water from dried mushrooms)
3	scallions, minced
½	tablespoon grated fresh ginger
	Kosher or sea salt
	Freshly ground pepper
	Roasted Potatoes (page 159)
	Lemon wedges, optional

Lightly brush the swordfish steaks with olive oil and season with salt and pepper and set them aside. In a large sauté pan, heat 3 tablespoons of the butter, and when it begins to foam, add the shallots and cook 1 to 2 minutes. Do not let them brown. Add the mushrooms and cook for 2 to 3 minutes, then add the wine and continue to cook until the liquid is reduced by two-thirds. Add the remaining butter, scallions, ginger, salt, and pepper. Keep warm while you grill the fish.

Grill the fish over a medium fire, 3 minutes a side. Place the grilled fish on a serving platter and top with a portion of the mushroom butter. Surround with the potatoes. Garnish with wedges of lemon if desired.

Here's another dish that was on our opening menu. We always serve
it with a side of Black Beans (page 163). The marinade, which has a really nice bright
summertime flavor, works well with pork, too. "Up" likes this dish a lot.
If you don't want to make your own achiote paste, it is available ready-made in some
Latin American markets. Use about 4 tablespoons of the ready-made paste.

SERVES 6

6 chicken breasts

Achiote Paste:

1½	teaspoons cumin seeds, toasted
½	teaspoon achiote (annatto seeds)
1	tablespoon marjoram or oregano
1	tablespoon chopped thyme
2	cloves garlic
	Kosher or sea salt
¼	teaspoon whole or freshly ground white peppercorns
3	tablespoons Chile Paste (page 226)
¼	cup fresh orange juice
1	teaspoon orange zest
¼	cup red wine vinegar
¼	cup olive oil
½	red onion, sliced thin
	Juice of 1 lime
½	cup sour cream
12	cilantro sprigs
	Black Beans (page 163)

Skin and bone the chicken breasts, and pound the meat to an even thickness. To make the achiote paste, with a mortar and pestle, or in a blender, grind up the cumin seeds, annatto seeds, marjoram, thyme, garlic, salt, and pepper. Make a marinade by combining the achiote paste with the Chile Paste, orange juice, zest, vinegar, and olive oil. Reserve half of the marinade for the sauce and spread the other half over the chicken and marinate for at least 2 hours.

Marinate the sliced onions in the lime juice at least 20 minutes to an hour. This will make them turn a bright pink.

Grill the chicken over a medium fire. Place the chicken on a serving plate, drizzle the reserved marinade over the chicken, and garnish with sour cream, marinated onions, and cilantro. Serve with Black Beans on the side.

Grilled Chicken Breast with Greens and Ginger-Mint Butter

The marinade gets some zip from the combination of the mustard and ginger. This also works well on chicken thighs if anyone is still eating dark meat anymore.

MAKES 6 SERVINGS

6   chicken breasts

Marinade:

2   tablespoons grated fresh ginger
¼   cup Dijon mustard
1   teaspoon freshly ground pepper
½   cup olive oil
2   tablespoons chervil

Ginger-Mint Butter:

6   tablespoons butter
2   teaspoons grated fresh ginger
1½   tablespoons chopped mint
   Pinch of kosher or sea salt
   Pinch of freshly ground white pepper

The Greens:

3   tablespoons butter
3   tablespoons minced shallots
12   cups greens (red chard, mustard, escarole, spinach, or kale)
1½-2 cups Chicken Stock (page 223)
⅓   cup balsamic vinegar
1   teaspoon kosher or sea salt
1   teaspoon freshly ground pepper

Skin and bone the chicken breasts. Combine the marinade ingredients and marinate the chicken breasts for at least 2 hours.

Combine all the ingredients for the Ginger-Mint Butter and set aside.

Over a medium hot fire, grill the chicken breasts, turning them to make nice grill marks on the surface.

While grilling the chicken, prepare the greens. Heat the butter in a large sauté pan, and add the shallots and greens. Sauté for 1 minute, then add the chicken stock. Cook until the stock is almost gone, stirring to allow the greens to cook evenly. You may have to cook in batches, depending on the size of your pan. Add the balsamic vinegar, salt, and pepper. Continue cooking for another minute.

Top each chicken breast with a dollop of the Ginger-Mint Butter, and serve with the greens and Mashed Potatoes (page 158), if desired.

"Chicken on a Bisquit" with Virginia Ham and Cream Gravy

Robert, the chef at the Diner, developed this dish. A creamy sauce chock full of diced
chicken breast, mushrooms, peas, and red bell pepper is a pleasing meal
for a cold winter's night. A nice green salad and some fruit would round out the meal.
Don't be afraid to change the vegetables depending on what's in season.
Bake the biscuits while making the gravy, keeping the oven warm to finish the dish.
You need enough ham to cover both halves of each biscuit.

SERVES 6

6	Buttermilk Biscuits (page 31)
2-2½ cups	Cream Gravy (recipe follows)
6-12	paper-thin slices Virginia ham
1-1¼ pounds	boneless chicken breast, cubed
1	tablespoon kosher or sea salt
1	teaspoon freshly ground white pepper
2	tablespoons olive oil
1	cup sliced wild mushrooms (chanterelles, hedgehogs, shiitake, or oyster mushrooms)
1	cup diced onion
½	cup heavy cream
¾	cup shelled sweet young peas
¾	cup diced roasted red bell pepper
2	tablespoons chopped dill
1½	tablespoons Chinese Mustard (page 169) or hot and sweet mustard
1½	tablespoons mayonnaise (page 169)

Bake the biscuits (page 31) and prepare the Cream Gravy (see recipe below).

Set the oven to 250 degrees. Sear the ham in a large nonstick or heavy sauté pan until lightly browned, and reserve on a platter in the oven. Sprinkle the chicken with salt and pepper. Add the olive oil to the same pan you used for the ham, and sauté the chicken until it is lightly browned. Reserve in the oven with the ham. Again using the same pan, cook the mushrooms and onions over medium heat until the onions are translucent and the mushrooms have given off some juice. Add the Cream Gravy, bring to a boil, reduce to a simmer, and cook 3 to 5 minutes to thicken. Add the cream and chicken, and heat through. Then add the peas and roasted red pepper, and cook until the peas are tender. Add a sprinkling of dill and taste for the seasoning.

While the vegetables are cooking, begin to assemble the serving plates. Combine the mustard and mayonnaise. Split the biscuits and lightly spread both halves with the mustard-mayonnaise.

Put a biscuit open-faced on each serving plate and cover the biscuits with ham. Pour the chicken and gravy over the ham and garnish with chopped dill.

Cream Gravy

4	tablespoons butter
¼	cup flour
4	cups Chicken Stock (page 223)
1	whole clove
1	small onion, peeled
1	bay leaf

In a heavy-bottomed saucepan melt the butter over medium heat. As soon as the butter begins to bubble (don't let it brown), add the flour and cook together for 1 to 1½ minutes. Slowly whisk the chicken stock into the butter-flour. Stick the clove into the onion and add to the sauce along with the bay leaf. Simmer for 30 minutes, stirring now and then, and skimming as needed. Remove the onion and bay leaf before using.

Chicken Curry Pot Pie

At the Diner we serve this in 4½-inch soufflé dishes, but small foil pot-pie
dishes will do the job, too. Boo and I both think this is our favorite
large plate . . . it's all self-contained so there's nothing else to distract you
from what you're eating. Be careful: these look so
tempting when they come out of the oven, it's easy to burn your mouth.
And they stay hot so long you can take them to a picnic.

SERVES 6

Crust:

1¼   cups flour
½   teaspoon sea salt
4   tablespoons butter
4   tablespoons vegetable
     shortening
2-3 tablespoons ice water

Chicken Filling:

⅓   cup olive oil
1¼   pounds chicken breast meat,
     diced
     Kosher or sea salt
     Freshly ground white pepper to
     taste
¾   pound crimini or shiitake mush-
     rooms, sliced
1   tablespoon toasted curry
     powder
½   pound carrots, peeled and
     diced
1   cup fresh corn kernels
1   cup shelled sweet young peas
½   pound potatoes, cooked and
     diced

2   cups Chicken Stock (page 223)
⅓   cup Cream Gravy (see
     preceding recipe)
2¼   cups heavy cream
1   tablespoon minced parsley

½   cup milk

Preheat oven to 375 degrees.

Put the flour and salt in a small mixing bowl and cut in the butter and shortening until the mixture is pea-sized. Add the water and quickly stir to form a dough. Form the dough into a log and chill at least 30 minutes. Remove from refrigerator and cut into 6 equal pieces. On a lightly floured surface, roll each piece into a 5½-inch-diameter circle. This allows a ½-inch overhang for each soufflé dish. Set aside.

Heat 4 tablespoons olive oil in a large sauté pan. Sauté the chicken in batches so as to not crowd it and so it turns a nice golden brown. Season with salt and pepper and distribute evenly between the soufflé dishes.

Add additional olive oil to the sauté pan if necessary and sauté the mushrooms. When they release their juices, add the curry powder and let it "bloom" for 1 minute. Add the vegetables and stir together to distribute the curry powder. Season with salt and pepper. Divide the vegetables evenly between the 6 soufflé dishes.

In the same pan combine the stock and Cream Gravy and reduce by one-third. Add the cream and reduce by half, then add the parsley and correct the seasoning. Pour equal amounts into the soufflé dishes and mix with the chicken and vegetables.

Top each dish with a circle of pie dough and brush with milk. Cut a few steam vent holes in the dough, place the soufflé dishes on a baking sheet, and bake for 15 to 20 minutes or until golden brown.

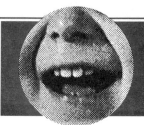

Grilled Rabbit with Ancho Chile Succotash

If you've never eaten rabbit, you should really give it a try. Rabbit has a flavor that is similar to chicken, but more interesting, and since rabbit is very low in fat, what can you lose? You can use the same marinade with chicken breasts or half chickens instead of the rabbit.

SERVES 6

3   rabbits

Marinade:

2	tablespoons chopped parsley
2	tablespoons chopped chives
1	tablespoon chopped chervil
2	tablespoons chopped shallots
2	tablespoons brandy
6	tablespoons Madeira
6	tablespoons olive oil
	Kosher salt or sea salt
	Freshly ground pepper

Ancho Chile Succotash (recipe follows)

3   tablespoons minced chives, for garnish

Cut the rabbits into 6 pieces: split them in half down the back, and remove the front and back legs. Debone the thighs, and cut the loin meat off the back bones. Depending on what else you are serving, you might want to save the front legs for a soup or stew at another meal.

Combine the marinade ingredients in a large mixing bowl and marinate the rabbit pieces for 6 to 24 hours in the refrigerator.

Remove the rabbit from the marinade and grill over a medium fire. Start with the back legs, as they take the longest to cook. Grill the back legs about 8 minutes, the front legs 5 to 6 minutes, and the loins for 4 to 5 minutes.

Place the rabbit on a serving plate, pour the succotash over it, and sprinkle with chives.

Ancho Chile Succotash

This is not a true succotash because the lima beans are missing. We use black-eyed peas because we can't get fresh limas—and I don't like lima beans anyway. Of course, if you do happen to like lima beans, feel free to substitute them for the peas. We always serve this with grilled rabbit, but it would also be good with grilled chicken or turkey.

½	cup black-eyed peas (or lima beans)
4	tablespoons unsalted butter
3	cloves garlic, minced
3	tablespoons minced shallots
⅓	cup roasted red bell pepper, diced
1¼	cups fresh corn kernels
1¼	cups shelled sweet young peas
2	cups Chicken Stock (page 223)
6	tablespoons Chile Paste (page 226)
¼	cup sherry vinegar
	Kosher or sea salt
	Freshly ground white pepper

Cook the black-eyed peas or limas in boiling water until tender, about 15 minutes. Melt 2 tablespoons of butter in a sauté pan and over medium-high heat, cook the garlic and shallots for 1 minute or until slightly browned. Add the red bell pepper and cook 1 minute more, then add the corn, peas, black-eyed peas (or lima beans) and cook 2 minutes more. Add the stock and reduce the liquid by half. Add the Chile Paste and sherry vinegar, and continue to reduce the liquid until the sauce has thickened. Stir in the remaining 2 tablespoons of butter and season with salt and freshly ground pepper.

Grilled New York Sirloin Steak with Mushroom Sauce and Bread Pudding

Be sure to select well-marbled steaks that weigh at least 8 ounces each. Anything smaller will be overdone on the inside before it caramelizes on the outside. You can make the sauce with any kind of mushrooms, but it will taste better if you use several different varieties. The Bread Pudding reminds me of a stuffing: it makes a nice change when you're tired of potatoes.

SERVES 6

6   dry-aged New York sirloin steaks (or tenderloins or rib eyes), 8 to 10 ounces each

Sauce:

5   tablespoons butter
1   cup sliced red onion (thin wedges)
2   cups mushrooms, cleaned and sliced (chanterelles, hedgehogs, morels, shiitake, or oyster mushrooms)
3   tablespoons Dijon mustard
⅓   cup balsamic vinegar
½   cup Chicken Stock (page 223)
    Kosher or sea salt
    Freshly ground pepper
    Bread Pudding (recipe follows)

Grill the steaks over a medium fire to desired doneness. While the steaks are grilling, melt 3 tablespoons of butter in a large sauté pan and sauté the red onion and mushrooms until they become slightly limp. Add the Dijon mustard and sauté for another 30 seconds, then add the balsamic vinegar and cook until almost evaporated. Add the chicken stock and cook for 1 minute; remove from heat and swirl 2 tablespoons of butter into the sauce. Add salt and pepper to taste.

Spoon the sauce on the plate and place the steak on top. Serve a spoonful of Bread Pudding alongside, and garnish with a few sprigs of watercress, if desired.

Bread Pudding

You need to plan ahead so that the pudding will be done when you're ready to serve the rest of the meal. The pudding needs 45 minutes to bake: it can be baked and held in a warm oven for up to 30 or 40 minutes, which allows a little flexibility in timing.

1   cup diced onion
1-2 teaspoons minced garlic
4   tablespoons butter
4   eggs
2   cups half-and-half
2   tablespoons chopped thyme
    Pinch of cayenne
1   teaspoon salt
½   teaspoon freshly ground pepper
8   cups 1-inch cubes French bread
1   cup grated cheddar cheese

Preheat oven to 375 degrees and butter a 9 x 13-inch baking pan. Sauté the onions and garlic in the butter until translucent. Beat the eggs in a large bowl. Add the half-and-half, thyme, cayenne, salt, and pepper and continue beating until completely incorporated. Pour the onion and egg mixture over the bread and grated cheese and mix well. Pour everything into the prepared pan, level it out, and bake for 45 minutes or until the top is golden brown and a knife inserted in the center comes out clean.

Grilled Skirt Steak with Wild West Steak Sauce

A skirt steak is a long 3-inch-wide strip of meat cut from the navel area.
It is usually very well marbled with fat, hence the flavor.
Old-time Jewish families in Chicago, where I first learned of it, called it
a skirt tenderloin. Outer skirt is the piece you want,
not inner skirt, which is too tough. The marinade works well with other
cuts such as tri-tips, rib eyes, or flank steaks.
This recipe is dedicated to Morgan Elizabeth Higgins because
it's her favorite dish.

SERVES 6

2½ pounds skirt steak

Marinade:

1   ½-inch piece of ginger, peeled and grated
4-6 cloves garlic, chopped
1   teaspoon freshly ground white pepper
2   tablespoons pure maple syrup
2   tablespoons soy sauce
2   tablespoons olive oil
2   tablespoons rice vinegar
1   tablespoon sesame oil

Wild West Steak Sauce (recipe follows)

Trim all the excess fat and sinew from the steak and cut it into 6 large or 12 medium-sized steaks, whichever is easier for you to handle that will look good on your plate. Stir all the marinade ingredients together in a low, flat container. Add the meat, making sure each piece is coated with the marinade on all sides. Marinate in the refrigerator for 2 to 4 hours.

If you marinate it longer, it will pick up more of the flavor of the marinade, but as the marinade permeates the meat, it will color it. When you cook the meat, it will appear well-done on the inside even when it is rare. If the color doesn't bother you, go ahead and marinate the meat longer.

Remove the meat from the marinade and bring to room temperature. Grill the steaks to desired degree of doneness and serve with a ramekin of Wild West Steak Sauce. This is good with french fries, or with mashed or baked potatoes (see the chapter on Sides and Condiments for recipes).

Wild West Steak Sauce

One day, our chef, Robert Cubberly, decided to make a steak sauce for the Diner, and this is what he came up with (after reading the ingredient lists on about 57 different kinds of commercially prepared steak

sauces). I like it with any cut of grilled steak. It can also be used with burgers, or in meat loaf.

1   tablespoon tamarind paste
2   tablespoons brown sugar
½   cup ketchup
⅓   cup ketjap manis or tamari soy sauce
1   papaya (or mango), peeled and seeded
1   teaspoon Chile Paste (page 226)
2   teaspoons chile powder
¼   cup rice vinegar
¾   cup water
1   teaspoon minced ginger
1   clove garlic, minced
½   teaspoon freshly ground pepper

Combine all the ingredients in a saucepan and simmer 30 minutes. Purée and chill.

"Up" said why don't you do something with less expensive cuts of meats, and here is what I came up with—short ribs braised in a sort of barbecue sauce. We use kosher-cut short ribs, which are cut 2 inches long and 6 inches wide across three ribs—each piece makes a neat single serving. You can make the ribs a day ahead and cook the peas and carrots separately when you reheat the short ribs and sauce. The vegetables will add a bright fresh element to the dish. Mashed potatoes are everyone's favorite with a sauce like this.

Serves 6

6	kosher-cut beef short rib sections
2	teaspoons salt
2	teaspoons freshly ground pepper
2	tablespoons olive oil

Braising Liquid:

2	tablespoons olive oil
3	onions, peeled and sliced (1¼ pounds)
12	cloves garlic, smashed
3	tomatoes, quartered (1¾ pounds)
3	cups Veal or Beef Stock (page 222) or water
3	cups barbecue sauce (one without liquid smoke)
10	sprigs thyme
½	teaspoon freshly ground pepper

Vegetables:

¾	pound sweet young peas, shelled
½	pound carrots, peeled and sliced
1	tablespoon butter
	Kosher or sea salt

Freshly ground pepper

Mashed Potatoes (page 158)
Chopped chives or parsley for garnish

Preheat oven to 325 degrees. Sprinkle the ribs with salt and pepper. Heat the olive oil in a large skillet and brown the ribs on all sides. Remove the ribs to a roasting pan or large casserole and drain off the oil.

To prepare the braising liquid, heat the olive oil, onion, and garlic in the skillet and sauté over medium-high heat for about 5 minutes, or until caramelized. Add the tomatoes and cook until soft, and then add the stock, barbecue sauce, thyme, and pepper. Bring to a boil and pour over the ribs. The ribs should be covered by the liquid: if necessary add water. Cover and bake for 1 to 1½ hours, until the meat is very tender and is shrinking away from the bones. Remove the meat from the sauce, arrange on a platter and keep warm until ready to serve. Strain the sauce and let stand for a few minutes. Skim off the fat that rises. If you are cooking this the day before, refrigerate the meat and sauce at this point. Before serving, remove the layer of fat from the sauce, and reheat it and the ribs together.

Combine the peas and carrots in a saucepan and add just enough water to be slightly visible but not to cover. Bring to a boil, and add the butter, salt, and pepper. The water will evaporate as the vegetables cook, leaving them nicely glazed.

Place the mashed potatoes on the serving plates and top with the ribs. Pour the sauce over the ribs and potatoes. Spoon the vegetables around the potatoes and meat. Garnish with chopped chives or parsley.

Calf's Liver with Apple-Smoked Bacon and Balsamic Onions

Except for the balsamic vinegar and thyme to dress up the onions, and the
homemade ketchup, this is just like the dish I grew up on.
You could serve it with the classic diner side of Mashed Potatoes (page 158),
but it would also go well with Polenta Cakes (page 160).
My mom always soaked the liver in milk for a bit before cooking it.
You could try that for a milder flavor.

SERVES 6

2½   pounds calf's liver
2   teaspoons olive oil
     Kosher or sea salt
     Freshly ground black pepper

Balsamic Onions:

2   tablespoons olive oil
3   medium-sized red onions, peeled
     and cut in wedges
2   tablespoons balsamic vinegar
1   teaspoon thyme
     Kosher or sea salt
     Freshly ground pepper

18   slices apple-smoked bacon
     Housemade Ketchup (page 168)
3   tablespoons chopped parsley

Remove any membranes from the
liver and cut it into serving-sized
slices. Lightly brush the liver with 2
teaspoons olive oil and season with
salt and pepper. Set aside.

Heat 2 tablespoons olive oil in
a large sauté pan and cook the
onions over low heat for 20 minutes,
until tender and beginning to
caramelize. Add the balsamic vinegar, thyme, salt, and pepper and
continue cooking until the vinegar
is absorbed. Keep warm.

Griddle or fry the bacon until
crisp, and drain well. Keep warm.
Grill or pan-fry the liver over
medium heat to the desired degree
of doneness. Cooking time will vary
depending on how hot your grill
is and how thick the slices of liver
are.

To serve, ladle some ketchup
down the side of the plate and
place a piece of the liver alongside
the ketchup. Top the liver with
some onions and 3 strips of bacon.
Sprinkle liberally with parsley.

Pork Chop with Ginger Applesauce

Pork chops are typical diner or roadhouse food. Our version is somewhat untraditional, though, because we serve the chops with a ginger-flavored applesauce, and marinate the meat in an Asian-style marinade. The marinade seals in all the juices and forms a nice crusty golden brown glaze when the chop grills. The chops go well with Mashed Potatoes (page 158) and Glazed Carrots (page 161).

SERVES 6

6   pork chops, 10 ounces each, frenched

Marinade:

Juice and zest of 1 orange
3   cloves garlic, peeled and mashed
1½   tablespoons peeled and grated ginger
⅔   cup ketjap manis (or ¼ cup molasses plus ½ cup tamari or dark soy sauce)
1½   tablespoons each light and dark soy sauce
⅓   cup rice vinegar
3   tablespoons olive oil
1   teaspoon freshly ground white pepper

Ginger Applesauce:

5   Pippin or Granny Smith apples, peeled, cored, and sliced
¼   cup sugar
     Juice and zest of 1 lemon
2   tablespoons sake
1   tablespoon peeled and grated ginger
     Pinch of cayenne

Glazed Carrots (page 161)
Mashed Potatoes (page 158)

Trim all fat and sinew from the pork chops. In a mixing bowl, thoroughly combine all the marinade ingredients. Coat the chops in the marinade and place in a low, flat nonaluminum container and let marinate for several hours or overnight.

To prepare the applesauce, place the apples, sugar, lemon juice and zest, and sake in a saucepan. Heat it not quite to the boiling point. Reduce heat to a simmer, cover, and cook until the apples are tender, about 15 minutes. Be careful not to scorch the apples. Mash the apples with the back of a wooden spoon—the sauce should be lumpy. Stir in the ginger and cayenne.

Grill the pork chops over a medium fire, turning them to make attractive grill marks. It will take about 12 to 15 minutes in all, as these are quite thick chops. Serve with 3 tablespoons of Ginger Applesauce for each serving, and the carrots and potatoes.

This is a really quick, simple, and colorful meal. The salsa can be done ahead; the pork and the beans both cook fast. If you want to round the meal out with a side dish, Potatoes Gratin (page 159) is a good choice.

SERVES 6

3   pork tenderloins, 12 ounces to 1 pound each

1   tablespoon olive oil
     Kosher or sea salt
     Freshly ground pepper

Tomato Salsa:

2   tablespoons rice vinegar
     Kosher or sea salt to taste
     Freshly ground pepper

⅓   cup olive oil

1   clove garlic, minced

4   scallions, minced

3   tomatoes, peeled, seeded and diced

1   roasted jalapeño, seeded and minced

2   tablespoons cilantro, minced

¾   pound fresh green beans

2   tablespoons butter
     Kosher or sea salt
     Freshly ground pepper

6   lime wedges

Trim the tenderloins of all fat and sinew. Rub the meat with the olive oil, salt, and pepper. To spice this up you could rub the pork tenderloins with some BBQ Pork Spice Blend, (page 226), too. Set aside until ready to grill. For the salsa, combine the vinegar, salt, and pepper and whisk in the oil. Gently stir in the remaining salsa ingredients.

Grill the pork tenderloins over a medium fire, turning so they cook evenly. While the pork is on the grill, cook the green beans in boiling water until tender. Drain and toss with butter and salt and pepper to taste.

Slice the pork tenderloins on the bias and place on individual serving plates. Top each serving with Tomato Salsa, arrange the green beans around, and garnish with a lime wedge.

Lamb Chops with Mint Sauce

My grandmother and mom are responsible for the mint sauce. When
we made it at home, we always chopped the mint in a
wooden bowl with a hand-held chopper that looked like a board scraper rounded
to fit the bowl. (The Italians have a tool like it called a *mezzaluna*,
a double-handled wizard of a thing used for chopping herbs.) Have your butcher
trim a rack of lamb and cut it into single bone chops. For heartier
appetites, you can have them cut double bone chops. Serve the chops with
Potatoes Gratin (page 159) or Polenta Cakes (page 160).

SERVES 4

12 lamb rack chops

Mint Sauce:

1   bunch (2 cups) mint leaves,
    washed and finely chopped
¼   cup sugar
¼   cup champagne vinegar
¼   cup water
    Pinch of freshly ground black
    pepper

    Kosher or sea salt
    Freshly ground black pepper

Trim the chops of all fat and sinew
and set aside. Combine the mint,
sugar, vinegar, water, and pepper
in a small bowl, and let stand 30
minutes to 2 hours before serving.

Season the chops with salt and
pepper. Grill over medium heat
about 2 minutes a side for rare, and
about 4 minutes for medium. Turn
while grilling to make attractive
grill marks. Serve on a plate with
the mint sauce in a ramekin, and
with Potatoes Gratin or Polenta
Cakes on the side.

Lamb Stew with Sweet Potatoes and Bell Peppers

Cooking the meat on the bone decreases shrinkage and creates a great
sauce that is infused with the flavor of lamb. You can bone the
shanks, or you can have a Flintstones party and serve the meat on the bone.
The lamb shanks can be prepared ahead of time, but since both
the meat and the vegetables are cooked in the oven, it might be easier
to just time it so they're both done about the same time.

SERVES 6

6	large lamb shanks
	Kosher or sea salt
	Freshly ground pepper
3	tablespoons olive oil
1	medium onion, quartered
8	garlic cloves
2	cups dry white wine
	Veal or Chicken Stock (pages 222 or 223), or water to cover shanks
5	sprigs thyme
3	bay leaves
1	tablespoon black peppercorns
2	sprigs fresh rosemary

Vegetables:

2	large sweet potatoes, peeled and cut into wedges
1	red bell pepper, seeded and cut in wedges
1	yellow bell pepper, seeded and cut in wedges
24	cloves garlic, peeled
1	large yellow onion, peeled and cut in wedges
2	tablespoons olive oil
3	tablespoons butter
¼	cup minced parsley for garnish
	Dutch Crunch Rolls (page 17)

Preheat oven to 375 to 400 degrees. Season the shanks with salt and pepper. Heat the oil in a heavy-bottomed pan and brown the lamb shanks until the meat caramelizes. Add the onion and garlic and continue to brown. Transfer the meat and onion to a large roasting pan or casserole. Deglaze the sauté pan with the wine, scraping up all the brown bits from the bottom of the pan. Pour the wine over the shanks and onions in the roasting pan or casserole and add enough stock or water to cover the shanks. Add 3 sprigs of thyme, bay leaves, and peppercorns. Bring to a boil on the stovetop, cover, and put it in the oven to braise for 1½ to 2 hours.

Remove the shanks from the broth; strain the broth and allow it to cool. If desired, remove the meat from the bones after it has cooled. Everything can be done ahead up to this point. To complete the preparation, skim off any fat from the broth. Add the rosemary, remaining thyme, salt, and pepper, and reduce the broth by half.

To prepare the vegetables, combine the sweet potatoes, peppers, garlic, wedges of onion, and olive oil, and roast covered in the oven for 30 minutes.

When ready to serve, melt the butter and lightly brown the lamb. Add the roasted vegetables and the reduced broth. Simmer until the sauce coats the vegetables and meat and everything is heated through, about 10 to 15 minutes. Serve in wide soup bowls garnished with parsley, and with plenty of Dutch Crunch Rolls for mopping up the sauce.

SIDES & CO

CHAP

NDIMENTS

TER 7

SIDES & CONDIMENTS
CHAPTER 7

In my family, mashed potatoes <u>are</u> the main dish. For most people, though, mashed potatoes, and other such side dishes, are meant to complement the main course. Feel free to mix and match the side dishes in this chapter, and use them as you like. Add a side of french fries and a side of cole slaw to the crab cakes, for instance, and you can end up with a large plate, or serve either one as a small plate.   We make most of our own condiments at the Diner, simply because, with few exceptions, there is just no comparison between homemade and store-bought stuff. The Tomato Chutney, Housemade Ketchup, and Bread and Butter Pickles are great to have in your fridge to add a bright spot to a simple sandwich, omelet, or grilled pork chop. Most of the condiments keep very well as long as they are stored in the refrigerator. I love being able to eat Tomato Chutney in the middle of January and getting a big old taste of summer. The chutney, by the way, is great on cheeseburgers, or grilled cheese sandwiches. Use it if you run out of ketchup and/or pickles.

French Fries

Everyone loves french fries, but Bill Upson's daughters, Lindsay and Alex, may be carrying it too far. This is all I have ever seen them eat! If you want to make good french fries, you have to have potatoes with the proper sugar/starch ratio. We use Kennebecs, which fry up crispy and golden brown. The problem with most supermarket potatoes, though, is that they've been held in cold storage (55 degrees or less), and under those conditions, the starch converts to sugar, and you get limp greasy fries. Yuck! For deep-fat-frying I prefer peanut oil. If you are only frying potatoes, the oil can be reused.

5   pounds potatoes, Kennebecs preferably
       Kosher or sea salt

Scrub the potatoes and cut them lengthwise. We use a 3/16-inch-square cutter, but you can cut them any size you like. Soak them in water to remove excess starch, and dry them.

Just before serving, heat the oil to 375 degrees and fry the potatoes in small batches until golden brown and crispy, about 3 minutes. Drain them on a cookie sheet and sprinkle with salt.

Thicker fries should be fried twice: fry them first at 325 degrees, for 5 to 8 minutes, remove them and drain them, and then fry them again at 375 degrees until the desired color and crispness are reached.

Mashed Potatoes

I like lumps, just a few—to let me know I'm eating real potatoes.

2   pounds russet potatoes (approximately 5 potatoes)
2   tablespoons butter, or more, cut in small pieces
⅓   cup milk, or less
      Kosher or sea salt
      Freshly ground pepper
      Extra butter (optional)
      Minced chives (optional)

Peel the potatoes and cut them into 1-inch pieces. Boil in salted water until tender but not mushy, about 20 minutes.

Drain the potatoes well and mash with a potato masher or, if you don't like lumps, a ricer. Add the butter in small pieces and stir in the milk gradually, being sure not to make the potatoes too loose. If the texture is right, don't add all the milk.

Season with salt and pepper. If desired, top each serving with more butter and a pinch of minced chives.

Potatoes Gratin

SERVES 6

Three thin but creamy, rich layers of potatoes. It's very important to cut the potatoes very thin so they absorb the cream and cook through without drying out.

2-3   large russet potatoes
¼   cup grated asiago cheese
1   cup cream
    Kosher or sea salt
    Freshly ground pepper

Preheat oven to 350 degrees. Butter a 9 x 13-inch baking pan. Peel the potatoes and slice them ⅛ inch thick by hand or on a mandoline. Rinse in cold water and dry. For each layer use one-third of the potatoes and lay them out slightly overlapping, sprinkle with one-third of the cheese and just enough cream to coat them, and then sprinkle with salt and pepper. Bake for 45 minutes to an hour.

Roasted Potatoes

SERVES 6

These are simple to prepare, and so delicious. In my house there are never any leftovers. For best results, use small new potatoes. If you can get them, try Yellow Finns, creamers, or Yukon Gold potatoes. You can also roast carrots by the same method; just peel them and cut them up, and follow directions for the potatoes.

18   small potatoes, quartered
3   tablespoons olive oil
1   tablespoon thyme
1½   teaspoons kosher or sea salt
½   teaspoon freshly ground pepper

Preheat oven to 400 degrees. Combine the potatoes and olive oil in a roasting pan, turning the potatoes so that they are coated with oil. Sprinkle on the thyme, salt, and pepper, and roast uncovered for 30 to 45 minutes or until fork tender and nicely browned. Stir occasionally during cooking.

Grilled Sweet Potatoes

SERVES 6

Since the sweet potato caramelizes so nicely, it is fun to grill. This is a good side dish to make when you already have the grill fired up to cook some other food. To speed this dish up, you can prebake or steam the sweet potatoes ahead of time, 15 to 25 minutes, depending on the size. Grill them just before serving to flavor them and heat them through.

3   large or 6 small sweet potatoes
    Olive oil
    Kosher or sea salt
    Freshly ground pepper

Slice the unpeeled sweet potatoes ½ inch thick. Brush with olive oil and lightly sprinkle with salt and pepper. Grill over a medium fire on both sides until the potatoes are tender and caramelized.

Steamed New Potatoes

James Beard always waxed poetic about new potatoes steamed in their jackets. I've always liked them, but I really went nuts the first year we had our garden. We got up one morning to dig potatoes and brought them back to the house. We lightly washed them and steamed them for 10 minutes or so. When they were done, we drizzled them with melted butter seasoned with tarragon and sprinkled them with salt and pepper. My favorite breakfast ever. James Beard was right.

Polenta Cakes

These cakes are more tender and also more delicious (and more fattening)
than the average griddled or grilled polenta cakes because
of the eggs, cheese, and butter. If you want firmer cakes or "diet" cakes,
leave out the eggs, cheese, and butter, and use additional
stock in place of the cream. The cakes can be formed ahead of time
and griddled or sautéed at the last minute.

SERVES 6

1	cup heavy cream
1	cup Chicken Stock (page 223) or water
1½	tablespoons butter
¼	teaspoon nutmeg
½-¾	teaspoon kosher or sea salt
¼	teaspoon freshly ground pepper
½	cup semolina
1	cup polenta (coarse-ground cornmeal)
½	cup grated cheese: Jarlsberg, asiago, cheddar, or any combination
1	egg
1	tablespoon chopped parsley
3	basil leaves, cut into a fine chiffonade
	Butter or olive oil for griddling or sautéing

In a large saucepan, combine the cream, stock, butter, nutmeg, salt, and pepper, and bring to a full rolling boil. Stir in the semolina and polenta and continue to cook over medium heat until the mixture thickens and is smooth and the polenta grains are tender (about 10 minutes).

Off the heat, add the grated cheese and egg, mixing thoroughly. Add the herbs once the mixture has cooled.

Form into cakes, using about ½ cup of polenta for each, and sauté or griddle in butter or olive oil until golden brown on both sides and heated through.

Glazed Carrots

2   pounds carrots
3   tablespoons unsalted butter or olive oil
    Kosher or sea salt
    Freshly ground white pepper
½-¾ cup Chicken Stock (page 223), water, or
    white wine
3   tablespoons brown sugar (optional)

Peel the carrots and cut them into sticks 2 inches
long and ¼ inch wide. Heat the butter or olive
oil in a large skillet or sauté pan. Sauté the carrots
over medium heat 1 to 2 minutes, until lightly
coated with the olive oil or butter. Season with salt
and pepper and add the stock, water, or wine.
Reduce until the carrots are glazed. Add the brown
sugar at the end if the carrots are not sweet enough.

Puréed Butternut Squash

1   medium butternut squash
3   tablespoons butter
3   tablespoons cream or milk
    Kosher or sea salt to taste
    Freshly ground pepper to taste
1   Freshly ground nutmeg to taste
½   cup broken seasoned pecans

Bake squash at 375 degrees until fork tender, about
40 minutes to 1 hour. Cut in half; scoop out and
discard seeds and fibers, and peel. Purée the flesh
in a food processor, run through a food mill, or
mash with a potato masher. Add the butter, cream,
salt, pepper, and nutmeg, and combine. To serve,
reheat 10 to 15 minutes in a 350-degree oven, and
garnish with pecans..

Cole Slaw

It's hard to make a cole slaw that will make everybody happy.
It's like apple pie—everyone has their own definition, and they'll usually say their
mom's was the best. We finally got one that passed the Bill and Bill test.
It's made with an old-fashioned boiled dressing that coats the shredded vegetables
well and stays nice for several hours without getting watery. Extra
dressing will keep well: just cover and refrigerate.

SERVES 6

½   head each red and green
     cabbage, shredded
¼   cup red onion sliced very thin
1   carrot, peeled and shredded

Cole Slaw Dressing:

2   egg yolks
1½   teaspoons Colman's mustard
     powder
¼   cup sugar
1   tablespoon flour
     Pinch of cayenne
1   teaspoon kosher or sea salt
½   cup cider vinegar
½   cup heavy cream
1   tablespoon poppy seeds
1   tablespoon finely grated
     horseradish

Combine the cabbage, onion,
and carrot in a large bowl and
refrigerate.

In the top of a double boiler off
heat, combine the yolks with the
mustard, sugar, flour, cayenne, and
salt. Whisk in the vinegar slowly
to insure no lumps. Place over
simmering water and cook, stirring,
for 30 seconds. Stir in the cream
and continue cooking over simmering water until thick, about 2 to 3
minutes, stirring constantly. Cool
and add the poppy seeds and
horseradish.

Using about half the dressing,
dress the cabbage. Add more if
needed—you don't want the cole
slaw to be too dry, but you
don't want it swimming
in dressing, either.

Black Beans

When we were opening Buckeye, Gordon Drysdale, the chef at Bix, came to
help us out. That's when I learned his trick of adding soy sauce
and cardamom to the black beans. I never would have thought of it,
but it's terrific. The beans are made in a two-step process:
if you want, you could do the initial cooking of the beans the day before.
If you don't have time to make the Chile Paste,
you can use additional chile powder.

SERVES 6

2	cups dried black beans (about 13 ounces)
1	small onion, diced
1	tablespoon olive oil
2	cloves garlic, minced
1	teaspoon cardamom
1	teaspoon cumin
½	teaspoon chile powder
	Freshly ground pepper
3	tablespoons soy sauce
½	large red bell pepper, diced
1	onion, diced
1	tablespoon olive oil
3½	cups Chicken Stock (page 223), Vegetable Stock (page 224), or water
1	teaspoon cumin
1	teaspoon cardamom
6	basil leaves cut into chiffonade
1	tablespoon Chile Paste (page 226)
	Juice of 1 lime
	Kosher or sea salt
	Freshly ground pepper

Wash the beans and check them
for stones. In a large pot, cook the
small diced onion in the olive oil
until soft and slightly browned.
Add the garlic, cardamom, cumin,
chile powder, and pepper, and cook
1 minute. Add the beans, soy sauce,
and enough water to cover the
beans, and bring to a boil. Reduce
to a simmer, and cook the beans
until they are tender. (Depending
on how fresh the beans are, it could
take anywhere from ½ hour to 1½
hours.) Drain and spread the beans
out on a cookie sheet to cool.

In a large pan, sauté the diced
pepper and second onion in the
olive oil until soft. Add the cooked
beans, stock or water, cumin,
cardamom, basil, and Chile Paste.
Cook until hot and saucy. Just
before serving, add the lime juice
and salt and pepper to taste.

Guacamole

This recipe can be doubled easily and is great with chips and salsa, or with a quesadilla. How do you tell when an avocado is ripe? The stem should wiggle easily, and the flesh should give slightly when gently squeezed.

1	large ripe avocado
¼	tomato, seeded and minced
1	small handful cilantro, minced
¼	small red onion, minced
	Juice of 1 lime
	Kosher or sea salt to taste

Cut the avocado in half and remove the seed. Scoop out the flesh with a spoon and mash it together with the rest of the ingredients, using the back of a fork.

Pesto

When basil is in season, pesto is the best. There are so many uses for pesto—on pasta, of course, but you can also use it as a flavor enhancer in soups, sauces, and dressings. I like to spread it on slices of good bread and make open-faced tomato sandwiches.

2	cups basil leaves
4	cloves garlic, peeled
½	cup grated parmesan cheese
½	cup olive oil

Place the basil, garlic, and parmesan cheese in a blender or processor. Begin to process, adding the oil slowly. Process to a smooth paste. You may also make the pesto using a mortar and pestle: mash the garlic, basil leaves, and parmesan cheese together, then slowly add the olive oil. The texture will be quite a bit coarser.

Bread and Butter Pickles

Another great snack to have on hand in the refrigerator. I like to use Kirby cucumbers for this because they're small—about the size of a quarter in diameter. The pickles will keep refrigerated for several months. For longer storage, they should be canned (follow manufacturer's processing instructions).

3½   pounds pickling cucumbers (Kirbys, preferably)
¾   pound onions
4   cups cider vinegar
2   cups water
4½   cups sugar
2   tablespoons kosher or sea salt
3   tablespoons yellow mustard seeds
2   tablespoons celery seeds
1   tablespoon dill seeds
1   tablespoon coriander seeds
1   tablespoon white peppercorns
1-2 bay leaves

Slice the cucumbers ¼ inch thick. Cut the onions into thin wedges and separate them. Put the cucumbers and onions in a large bowl or stainless steel pot, cover with ice water, and soak for at least 1 hour.

Put the remaining ingredients in a stainless steel pot and bring to a boil. Drain the pickles and onions, place them back in the large bowl or pot and pour the hot liquid over them. Stir well. Weight the pickles down with a plate to insure they are all submerged in the liquid. Let sit for 24 hours in the refrigerator before using.

Tomato Chutney

You can use any type of tomato for this chutney—just select the ones with the best flavor and color. If you're lucky enough to get gold or yellow tomatoes, use currants in place of the golden raisins. This will give you a nice color contrast.

3-3½ pounds tomatoes, peeled and cut into chunks
1½   cups sugar
1   2-inch piece of ginger, peeled and grated
1   head garlic, peeled and minced (approximately 20 cloves)
1½   teaspoons cayenne
1½   cups cider vinegar
1½   teaspoons kosher or sea salt
¼   cup golden raisins

Combine all the ingredients except the raisins in a heavy-bottomed stainless steel pot. Simmer over low heat until thick, stirring occasionally so the chutney doesn't burn on the bottom of the pan. This could take anywhere from 30 minutes to 1 hour, depending on the water content of the tomatoes. The tomatoes should still be chunky. Don't stew them so long that they turn to mush, or you'll end up with something like a jam.

Add the raisins and cook 10 minutes longer. Cool before using. Keep refrigerated.

Pickled Onions

YIELDS 1 1/2 CUPS

Even though they are cooked, these onions still stay crunchy. They have a nice sweet-and-sour flavor, and go well with ham, smoked salmon, and, of course, hot dogs.

2	tablespoons olive oil
3	onions, sliced into thin wedges
¼	cup red wine vinegar
¼	cup sugar
½	teaspoon kosher or sea salt
1	tablespoon ketchup
	Pinch each of cayenne and black pepper

Heat the olive oil in a medium saucepan over medium-low heat. Add the onion slices, stir, cover, and cook slowly until tender, but not soft and mushy, 15 to 20 minutes. Do not allow the onions to brown. Add the remaining ingredients and bring to a boil. Reduce to a simmer and cook for 3 minutes. Remove from heat and cool. Store leftovers in the refrigerator.

Pickled Ginger

When you make pickled ginger, you might as well put up a large batch. It keeps well and is good with a lot of things. I find that Japanese mandolines are the best tool for thinly slicing ginger; use the hand guard and be careful!

1	pound ginger
1	cup rice vinegar
½	cup sugar

Peel the ginger and cut it lengthwise in 3- to 4-inch-long paper-thin slices. Put the ginger, vinegar, and sugar in a pot, bring to a boil, reduce heat, and simmer 5 minutes. Let cool. Keep refrigerated.

Housemade Ketchup

YIELDS 5 1/2 CUPS

We started making our own ketchup when I found a recipe for it in an old cookbook my grandmother used to use. The original recipe was way too heavy in cloves, so it evolved into this. We do use commercial ketchup at times (I think Heinz ketchup is the best), but we serve Housemade Ketchup with hamburgers, plain hot dogs, french fries, onion rings, and the calf's liver. This recipe works best with vine-ripened tomatoes: if you grow your own, it's a good way to use them up if too many ripen at once.

6½	pounds tomatoes, peeled, seeded, and finely chopped
1	teaspoon kosher or sea salt
2	cups sugar
1	whole clove
3	bay leaves
½	teaspoon ground coriander
¼	stick cinnamon
1	tablespoon Colman's mustard powder
2	large cloves garlic, minced
½	teaspoon freshly ground black pepper
1½	cups cider vinegar
	Dash of cayenne

Combine all the ingredients in a heavy-bottomed stainless steel pot. Bring to a good rolling boil, stirring occasionally. Reduce to a simmer and cook about 45 minutes, until thick, being very careful not to scorch the sauce.

Chinese Mustard

YIELDS 1 1/2 CUPS

A bit of this mixed with mayonnaise is great with ham or turkey sandwiches.

1	cup sugar
½	cup Colman's mustard powder
4	egg yolks
1	cup red wine vinegar

Mix the sugar and mustard together in the top part of a double boiler, not over heat. Whisk the egg yolks and vinegar together in a small bowl. Add them to the sugar and mustard, and whisk until the mixture is completely smooth. Cook over simmering water in the double boiler, whisking occasionally, until the mixture thickens. Remove from heat and cool. Store covered in the refrigerator.

Crème Fraîche

YIELDS 1 1/4 CUPS

Commercially made crème fraîche is available in supermarkets, but it is so easy to make you should try it at least once. Refrigerated, it will keep about a week to ten days. Swirl a little into this or that; or whip it and add a dollop to a soup or stew. Sweeten it and use it like whipped cream

¼	cup buttermilk
1	cup heavy cream

Thoroughly mix the cream and buttermilk and let it sit at room temperature, loosely covered, for 8 to 12 hours until thick. Keep refrigerated.

Mayonnaise

YIELDS 2 CUPS

There is some concern over egg safety in homemade mayonnaise, so you may prefer to buy it rather than make it. If you choose to buy mayonnaise, compare the different brands and settle on one that tastes best to you. Some of them have excessive amounts of sugar, salt, or mustard, so you'll need to adjust the seasonings in the recipes you use them in. If you choose to make your own, follow the simple directions below.

2	egg yolks
1	tablespoon rice or champagne vinegar
1	teaspoon Dijon mustard
	Tiny pinch of kosher or sea salt
	Freshly ground pepper
1-1¼ cups olive oil	

Whisk together the egg yolks, vinegar, mustard, salt, and pepper in a medium-sized bowl. Slowly whisk in the olive oil until thick. If you use a blender, blend together the egg yolks, vinegar, mustard, salt, and pepper first. Then, with the blender running, slowly add the olive oil until the mayonnaise thickens.

If the mayonnaise seems too thick, stir in a little cold water. If it tastes of eggs, thin it with a little cold water and slowly whisk or blend in a little more oil.

DESS

CHAP

ERTS

TER 8

We've probably stayed closest to the traditional American diner fare with our desserts. They're all big, gooey, and fattening, with lots of powdered sugar sprinkled over everything to top it off. My philosophy of desserts is very simple—if you're going to eat them at all, then make sure you eat the real stuff—real butter, real eggs, real vanilla, and so on. I would far rather eat a one-inch-square brownie made from real ingredients than some fake low-calorie thing ten times its size. I recommend you seek out the best chocolate, butter, and cream available in your area. It does make a difference in flavor, and for all those calories, you deserve great flavor.   I like to use vanilla beans rather than vanilla extract in making custards, puddings, and sauces. When you buy vanilla beans, look for plump, supple ones. To use them, split the pod and scrape out the tiny black seeds into whatever it is you are cooking. Sometimes I add the pod to the pot, too, then scrape it again after it has heated up. This is especially good to do if your vanilla beans are old and stiff. They soften up as they're heated, and you will get more out of the pod when you scrape it the second time. When the recipe calls for vanilla extract, be sure to use a good-quality extract.   In general, desserts are made by very specific formulas, and simply adding a little more or a little less of an ingredient, substituting ingredients, or increasing or decreasing the heat may change things drastically. Sometimes this will be for the better, but more often than not it won't. It's best to read through the entire recipe before you begin, so you have the whole picture before you start, then follow the recipe carefully, at least the first time you try it. If you do, you'll find that making desserts is a snap.

Chocolate Pecan Brownie à la Mode with Chocolate Sauce

These brownies are a favorite at the Diner, so they are always on the menu.
Bill Upson's wife Paula likes them a lot—she's one of
those lucky people who could eat a thousand of them and never gain an ounce.
Don't overmix or overcook these brownies or they'll become too
cakelike, and dry. They're supposed to be moist and gooey inside, so you can't test
them for doneness with a toothpick. Instead, keep an eye
on them while they're baking: they will swell up and then level off just
before they're done.

MAKES 12 LARGE BROWNIES

1	cup unsalted butter
4	ounces unsweetened chocolate, roughly chopped
1½	cups sugar
½	cup light corn syrup
1	teaspoon vanilla extract
½	teaspoon kosher or sea salt
3	eggs
1	cup flour
1	cup chopped toasted pecans
¾	cup semisweet chocolate chunks
	Vanilla ice cream
1	cup Chocolate Sauce (recipe follows) Sliced strawberries Powdered sugar

Preheat the oven to 350 degrees. Butter and flour a 9 x 13-inch cake pan.

In double boiler or a small bowl set over simmering water, melt half the butter and the unsweetened chocolate. Set aside to cool slightly. In a mixing bowl, cream together the remaining butter and the sugar. Beat in the syrup, vanilla, and salt. Beat in the eggs, one at a time. Stir in the melted chocolate mixture, and then the flour. Do not overmix. Stir in the pecans and chocolate chunks.

Spread the dough evenly in the prepared pan and bake at 350 degrees for 25 to 30 minutes. The brownies will swell up and then level off just before they are done. They should remain moist even when done: do not overbake.

Cool before cutting. To serve it as we do at the Diner, place a scoop of vanilla ice cream in the center of the brownie, and drizzle with warm Chocolate Sauce. Garnish with berries and dust with powdered sugar.

Chocolate Sauce

I eat this sauce by the spoonful when I am suffering from the blues. Not a great habit for my hips, but it always seems to cheer me up. I don't know if it's the sugar, or the caffeine, or both.

We use Guittard chocolate because it's a reasonably priced, good-quality chocolate. Also, it's made in Burlingame, which is not too far from San Francisco, and we like to use local products. This sauce keeps very well in the refrigerator. If you leave out the cream, it makes a great icing.

8	ounces semisweet chocolate (preferably Guittard's French Vanilla)
½	cup unsalted butter
2	tablespoons brandy or cognac
1	tablespoon triple sec
¾	cup light corn syrup
¾	cup heavy cream

Cut the chocolate and butter into small pieces and place with the brandy, triple sec, and corn syrup in a double boiler and allow to soften. The butter will melt, but the chocolate chunks will hold their shape until pressed. Remove from the heat and whisk together. When the mixture is smooth, stir in the cream.

Meghan Rhea's German Chocolate Cake with Coconut-Pecan Frosting

Meghan Rhea, who used to be the baker at Fog City Diner, left us
this wonderful cake recipe. We both used to make this cake for our dads—
for some reason, her cakes would always turn out better than mine!
This is one dessert that just screams for a tall glass of milk.

MAKES A 9-INCH DOUBLE-LAYER CAKE

1	cup unsalted butter, softened
2	cups sugar
½	teaspoon salt
1½	teaspoons vanilla extract
4	ounces semisweet chocolate, broken into pieces or chopped
½	cup boiling water
4	large eggs, separated
2½	cups cake flour
1	tablespoon baking soda
1	cup buttermilk

Garnish:

	Coconut-Pecan Frosting (recipe follows)
1½	cups toasted coconut
12	pecan halves, toasted

Preheat oven to 350 degrees. Butter and flour the sides of two 9-inch round cake pans and line the bottoms with parchment paper.

Using a mixer fitted with the paddle attachment, cream together the butter, sugar, salt, and vanilla until light and fluffy. Put the chocolate in a small bowl, pour the boiling water over it, and stir until smooth. Add to the butter mixture and beat until thoroughly combined. Beat the egg yolks into the batter, one at a time. In a separate bowl sift together the flour and baking soda, and add to the batter, alternating with the buttermilk. Beat the egg whites to soft peaks and fold into the batter.

Pour the batter into the prepared pans and bake for 40 minutes. Cool on a rack and remove from pans. When completely cool, fill and frost the cake. Use the toasted coconut to decorate the sides of the cake, and the pecan halves to decorate the top.

Coconut-Pecan Frosting

In order to get the proper consistency, this frosting has to be beaten for a long time, so I recommend you use an electric mixer.

1	cup dark brown sugar
1	cup heavy cream
8	egg yolks
1½	cups untoasted unsweetened coconut
1½	cups toasted chopped pecans
1½	teaspoons vanilla extract
2	cups unsalted butter, softened

In a small saucepan, bring the sugar and cream to a boil. In a medium-sized mixing bowl whisk the yolks together, then slowly whisk in one-fourth of the hot cream mixture (don't dump it all in at once or the yolks will cook). Slowly whisk in the remaining cream mixture. Return this to the saucepan, and cook slowly over low heat, stirring constantly, until thick enough to coat the back of a spoon. Place this mixture back in a mixing bowl and with a whisk, beat in the untoasted coconut and the pecans. Mix 8 to 10 minutes until cool. On medium speed, beat in the vanilla and the butter, 1 tablespoon at a time.

Lemon-Almond Pound Cake

In the summer this is nice with the Fruit Compote from the
Mixed Berry Parfait (page 201) or with ice cream and fresh berries. You can always
top it all off with lightly sweetened whipped cream.

MAKES ONE 9-INCH CAKE

1	cup blanched almonds
1	cup sugar
1	cup unsalted butter, softened
4	eggs
1	tablespoon grated lemon zest
1	cup flour
1	teaspoon baking powder
¼	teaspoon salt
¼	cup lemon juice

Lemon Glaze:

1   cup sifted powdered sugar dissolved in 2 tablespoons lemon juice

Preheat oven to 350 degrees. Butter and flour a 9-inch round cake pan, and line it with parchment paper.

Put the almonds and sugar in a processor and grind to a fine powder. Using an electric mixer, cream the butter, sugar, and almonds together until light and fluffy. Beat in the eggs one at a time, and mix in the lemon zest. Sift the flour, baking powder, and salt together into a separate bowl. Beat in the dry ingredients alternately with the lemon juice, about one-third of each at a time. Mix until thoroughly combined.

Pour the batter into the cake pan and bake for 50 minutes or until a wooden toothpick inserted in the center comes out clean. Cool completely and remove from the pan. Pour Lemon Glaze over the top and sides.

Gingerbread with Applesauce

I love the aroma of gingerbread baking in the oven. It makes me
feel all warm and safe. We always use fresh ginger in our gingerbread—
it makes all the difference in the taste. If you can't find it,
use candied or preserved ginger as a substitute rather than the dried
powder, which is often just like dust.
Gingerbread is great—with coffee in the morning, with tea
in the afternoon, or even as the whole meal. When you make it, try to time
it so that the gingerbread will still be warm from the oven when
you serve it. We glaze it with a lemon icing and serve it with homemade
applesauce. Gilding the lily, I think is what they call it.

SERVES 8

3	cups flour
1½	teaspoons baking powder
2	teaspoons cinnamon
½	teaspoon ground cloves
¼	teaspoon salt
1½	teaspoons baking soda
1½	cups boiling water
½	cup unsalted butter
1	cup sugar
1	cup molasses
2	tablespoons grated ginger
2	eggs

Lemon Glaze (see preceding recipe)
Applesauce (recipe follows)

Preheat oven to 325 degrees. Butter and flour a 9 x 13-inch baking pan. Sift the flour, baking powder, cinnamon, cloves, and salt into a medium-sized bowl. Dissolve the baking soda in the boiling water. Using the paddle attachment on a mixer, cream the butter and sugar together until light and fluffy. Beat in the molasses and ginger, and scrape down the sides of the bowl. With the mixer set to a slow speed, add the dry ingredients alternately with the baking soda water, about one-third of each at a time, scraping down the sides of the bowl. Mix in the eggs thoroughly, continuing to scrape down the sides of the bowl. The batter will be thin, but don't worry about it. Pour the batter into the prepared baking pan and bake 25 to 30 minutes or until a toothpick comes out clean. Cool in the pan.

Drizzle Lemon Glaze over the warm gingerbread. Serve it warm with a little applesauce or, if you prefer, with a dollop of lightly sweetened whipped cream and a sprig of mint.

Applesauce

Because this sauce was designed to be served with the gingerbread, it is quite tart. If you want a sweeter sauce, just add a little more sugar. I have made it with maple sugar instead of granulated sugar, and it was quite good. We use Pippin, Gravenstein, Macintosh, or Fuji apples, depending on the season.

4	apples, peeled, cored, and cut into ½-inch dice
¼	cup sugar
	Juice of 1 lemon
1	1-inch piece of vanilla bean

Put the apples, sugar, and lemon juice in a medium-sized pot. Split the vanilla bean pod in half lengthwise, scrape the seeds into the saucepan, and drop the pod in, too. Cover, and cook over low heat until the apples are tender. Usually 10 to 15 minutes will do it. Remove the bean pod, scrape it a second time, and discard.

Black and White Cheesecake

You get the best of both here—a chocolate cheesecake
and a vanilla-flavored cheesecake, all in one. If you want,
you can top it off with lightly sugared raspberries.

MAKES ONE 10-INCH CAKE

Chocolate Graham Cracker Crust:

1½	cups graham cracker crumbs
¼	cup sugar
3	tablespoons cocoa powder
½	cup butter, melted

Filling:

1½	pounds cream cheese
1	cup plus 2 tablespoons sugar
2	tablespoons flour
1	teaspoon grated lemon zest
1	teaspoon grated orange zest
3	whole eggs plus 2 yolks
½	teaspoon vanilla extract
6	ounces semisweet chocolate, melted
3	tablespoons heavy cream

Preheat oven to 325 degrees. Toss the crust ingredients together in a bowl. Press firmly into a 10-inch springform pan, and set aside.

Beat the cream cheese and sugar together until light and fluffy. Beat in the flour and zests, then slowly beat in the eggs, extra yolks, and vanilla. In a separate bowl, combine the melted chocolate and cream. Pour two-thirds of the cheesecake filling over the crust. Fold the chocolate mixture into the remaining filling until thoroughly combined. Using a knife, swirl the chocolate filling into the plain filling to get a marbled effect. Bake for 40 minutes. Turn off the oven, open the door, and let the cake stand for 20 more minutes inside the oven. Cool on a rack. Refrigerate overnight. To make neat slices, cut the cheesecake with a hot knife, rinsing it off between each cut.

Strawberry Rhubarb Crisp

Strawberries and rhubarb are two of the first signs of spring,
unless, of course, you live in California. This year in February
we got some of the best rhubarb I've had in years.

SERVES 8

4 cups strawberries, hulled and quartered
4 cups rhubarb, cut into ½-inch pieces
½ cup granulated sugar
1 tablespoon cornstarch
½ teaspoon cinnamon
Zest of 1 orange, finely grated
1 tablespoon brandy

Topping:

½ cup granulated sugar
½ cup brown sugar
1 cup unsalted butter, softened
½ teaspoon salt
1 teaspoon vanilla extract
1 teaspoon cinnamon
2 cups flour
½ cup rolled oats
1 cup blanched almonds, toasted and coarsely chopped

Preheat oven to 375 degrees. Butter a 9 x 13-inch baking pan. Place the strawberries and rhubarb in a large bowl. Mix together the sugar, cornstarch, and cinnamon and add it to the fruit along with the orange zest and brandy.

For the topping, combine the sugars, butter, salt, vanilla, and cinnamon in a medium-sized bowl. Add the flour, oats, and almonds and mix until crumbly.

Spread the fruit in the baking pan, cover it evenly with two-thirds of the topping, and bake for 15 minutes. Sprinkle the remaining topping over the top and bake another 15 minutes, until the fruit is bubbling and the top is golden brown and crisp. Serve warm—with some vanilla ice cream, if you like.

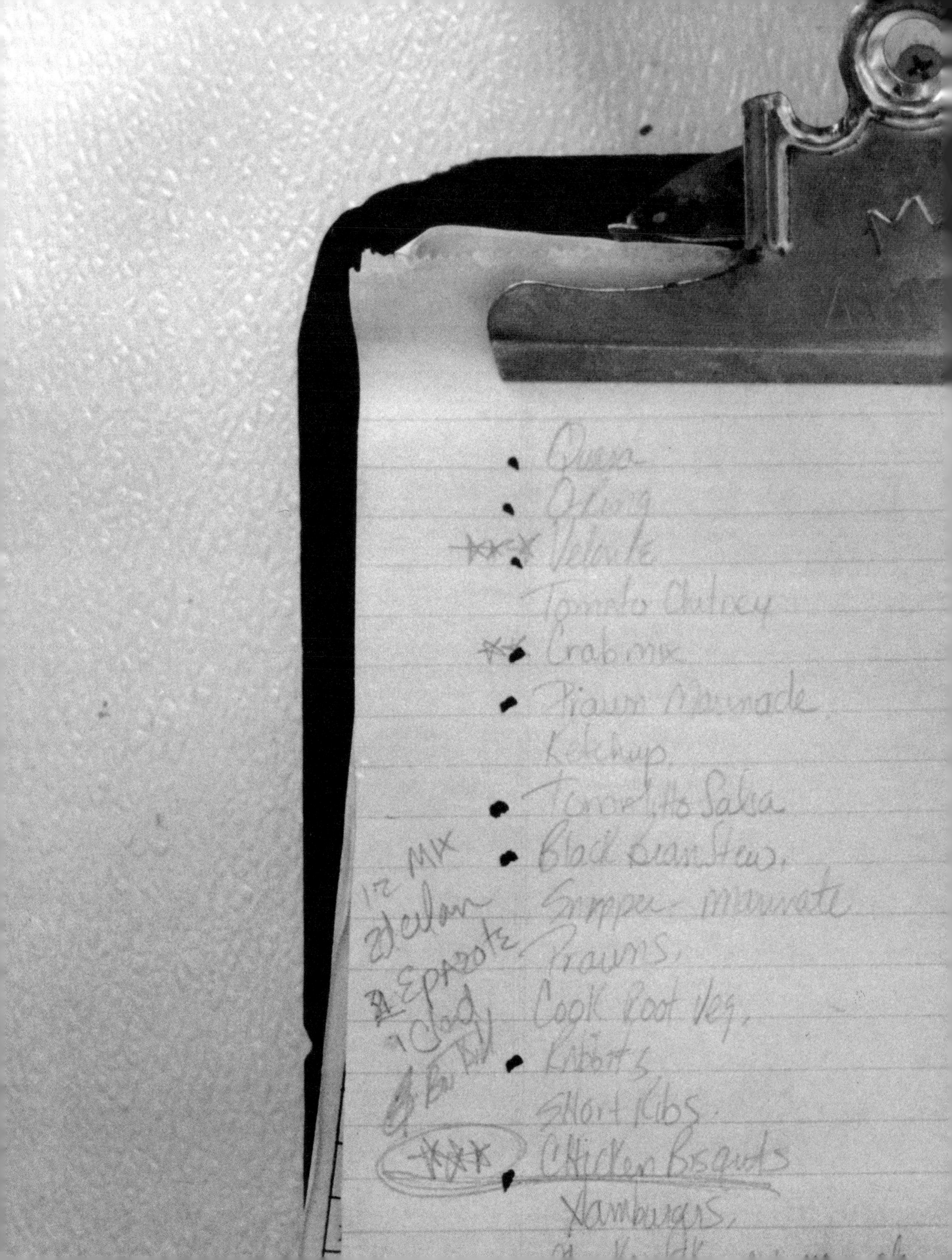

- Quesa
- Oring
★★ Delate
- Tomato Chutney
★★ Crab mix
- Prawn Marinade
- Ketchup
- Tomatillo Salsa
- Black Bean Stew

1) MIX
2) Helon — Snapper marinate
3) EPAZOTE Prawns,
Clove — Cook Root Veg.
Bay Leaf — • Rabbit 3
Short Ribs
(★★★) • Chicken Bisquits
Hamburgers

BAKESHOP WOULD
REALLY APPRECIATE:

- Peaches
- Scallions
- Japalenoes
- Corn

THANKS!

1 SILK pie in for right
reading in Bake shop

Peach and Blueberry Cobbler

Best served warm. Definitely one of those "comfort" foods that everyone seems to be talking about these days. You can peel the peaches or not, as you wish. The cornmeal in the topping gives this cobbler a little different taste. A planning tip: the cornmeal has to soak in the buttermilk for an hour before you can proceed with the recipe.

SERVES 8

Cornmeal Topping:

¼	cup coarse-ground cornmeal (polenta)
1	cup buttermilk
1	cup unsalted butter
⅓	cup sugar
1	teaspoon grated orange zest
1	egg
1¾	cups flour
1	teaspoon baking soda
1	teaspoon baking powder
¼	teaspoon salt

Filling:

8	cups fresh peaches, peeled and sliced ¼ inch thick
2	cups fresh blueberries
¾	cup sugar
1	tablespoon flour
¼	teaspoon nutmeg
¼	teaspoon cinnamon
½	teaspoon vanilla extract
1	tablespoon lemon juice

Stir the cornmeal and buttermilk together and set aside for 1 hour.

Preheat oven to 350 degrees. Butter a 9 x 13-inch baking pan. Using a mixer, cream the butter and sugar together until light and fluffy. Add the zest and the egg and beat until well mixed. Sift the flour, baking soda, baking powder, and salt into a separate bowl. With the mixer on low speed, add the dry ingredients alternately with the buttermilk mixture about one-third of each at a time.

In a large bowl, toss together all the filling ingredients. Place in the baking pan, and spread the topping evenly over the fruit all the way to the edges of the pan.

Bake for 45 to 50 minutes until topping is baked through. It's a good idea to put either a baking sheet or foil under the cobbler while it is baking to catch any juices that may bubble over.

Apple Dumplings

I have never used any other recipe for apple dumplings since I got this
one from Mary Johnson Tradewell, my roommate and best friend
in college. Mary grew up in Elbow Lake, Minnesota, and her mother,
Dames, was the original source for this recipe. Use tart apples—
poaching them in the cinnamon syrup will make them sweet.
The pastry is very delicate and the colder it is, the easier it is to work
with. You can also make this with peaches and plums.

SERVES 6

Poaching Liquid:

1½	cups water
1½	cups sugar
¼	teaspoon cinnamon
¼	teaspoon nutmeg
3	tablespoons unsalted butter

Dough:

2	cups flour
2	teaspoons baking powder
1	teaspoon kosher or sea salt
⅔	cup shortening
½	cup milk

Filling:

6	apples, peeled and sliced
⅓	cup sugar
	Pinch of cinnamon
	Pinch of nutmeg

Preheat oven to 375 degrees.

In a saucepan, bring the water, sugar, cinnamon, and nutmeg to a boil, add the butter, and remove from heat. Set aside.

Sift the flour, baking powder, and salt into a mixing bowl. Cut in the shortening until the mix is crumbly. Add the milk all at once and quickly stir in to bind. Thoroughly mix and form a dough. On a floured surface, roll the dough out into a rectangle about 12 x 18 inches, and about ⅛ inch thick. Cut the dough into six 6-inch squares.

In a mixing bowl, toss the apples with the sugar, cinnamon, and nutmeg. Divide the apples evenly among the squares of dough, bring up the edges of each square, and pinch together to enclose the apple mixture. Place the dumplings 1 inch apart in a 9 x 13-inch baking pan. Pour the poaching liquid over the dumplings and bake in the oven for 35 minutes, or until well browned.

Serve with some of the poaching sauce. Hot is best. A little vanilla ice cream or lightly whipped unsweetened cream would also be good.

Free-Form Apple Pie

When we were getting the Diner ready to open, there was so much
confusion that I forgot to order pie pans, and didn't realize it
until the very last minute. We had to have apple pies for our opening,
though, because they were on the menu, and besides,
what's a diner without apple pie? This pie was my solution.
Our favorite apples are ones that get soft and tender but not mushy,
and that have a sweet-tart flavor—Pippins, Gravensteins,
Macintoshes, and Granny Smiths are all good. The semolina crust
is a variation I made at home once when I ran out of flour.
It tasted good, so I thought I should include that option here.

MAKES 1 PIE

Pie Crust:

1½	cups flour, or
	1 cup flour and ½ cup semolina
½	teaspoon salt
1	teaspoon sugar
½	cup plus 2 tablespoons cold unsalted butter, diced
2-3	tablespoons ice water

Filling:

6-7	apples, peeled and sliced (7 cups)
2	tablespoons fresh lemon juice
½	cup sugar
1	teaspoon cinnamon
1	egg white
2	tablespoons unsalted butter

Combine the flour, (and semolina, if you're using it), salt, and sugar in a medium-sized bowl. Cut the butter into the flour until the mixture is the size of small peas. Sprinkle in the ice water and mix lightly until the dough comes together. Press the dough into a disk, cover it with plastic wrap, and chill for 30 minutes.

Preheat the oven to 400 degrees and butter a cookie sheet. Toss the apples with the lemon juice in a mixing bowl. Combine the sugar and cinnamon and reserve 1 tablespoon. Add the rest to the apples, and toss again.

Roll out the dough on a floured surface into an 18-inch circle. Place the dough on the prepared baking sheet and mound the apples in the center. Fold the dough up towards the center, pleating the dough as you go, and leaving a 2-inch hole in the center. Brush the top and sides with egg white to seal, and sprinkle with the reserved cinnamon sugar. Place 2 tablespoons of butter in the center hole.

Bake at 400 degrees for 15 minutes, then reduce heat to 350 degrees and bake for a further 30 to 40 minutes, or until the apples are tender and the juices are bubbling.

Pumpkin Pie

This is your basic Thanksgiving pumpkin pie, made with the fresh
pumpkins that are in season here between September
and December. To cook pumpkin, cut it in half and remove the seeds
and strings. Bake it cut side down at 350 degrees until fork
tender, about 45 minutes to an hour. We always use fresh ginger. If you
are unable to find fresh ginger, you might want to try
preserved or crystallized ginger. You can also substitute cooked
squash or sweet potatoes for the pumpkin.

MAKES TWO 9-INCH PIES

2	unbaked pie crusts (page 203)
2½	cups cooked pumpkin, cooled and puréed
1¼	cups dark brown sugar
1	teaspoon kosher or sea salt
½	teaspoon grated fresh ginger
2	teaspoons cinnamon
4	eggs, lightly beaten
2	cups heavy cream
1	teaspoon vanilla extract

Preheat oven to 400 degrees. Prepare the pie crusts and set aside.

In a large mixing bowl, combine the pumpkin purée, sugar, salt, ginger, and cinnamon, and mix together. Then add the eggs, cream, and vanilla, and mix thoroughly.

Pour the mixture into the pie crusts and bake in the oven for 45 to 50 minutes or until an inserted knife comes out clean.

Banana Cream Pie

This is a Diner classic. We make it with a chocolate-coated pie crust, which helps to keep it from getting soggy. Still, you should prepare the pie the same day that you plan to serve it, as it will not hold overnight. Add the whipped cream right before serving.

MAKES ONE 9-INCH PIE

1	9-inch Chocolate-Coated Pie Crust (page 203)
½	cup sugar
	Pinch of salt
4	teaspoons cornstarch
4	teaspoons flour
4	egg yolks
2	cups milk
1	2-inch piece of vanilla bean
1	teaspoon brandy
2	tablespoons unsalted butter
3	ripe bananas, sliced
1½	cups heavy cream
2	tablespoons sugar
½	teaspoon vanilla extract
1	bar semisweet chocolate (preferably Guittard's French Vanilla), room temperature, for garnish

Prepare the pie shell and chill it in the refrigerator.

In a medium-sized bowl, combine the sugar, salt, and cornstarch. Add the egg yolks and beat until smooth. Put the milk in a small saucepan. Split the vanilla bean pod in half lengthwise, scrape the seeds into the saucepan, and drop the pod in, too. Bring the milk to a boil. Whisk about ½ cup of the hot milk into the egg yolk mixture. Pour the warmed egg yolks back into the remaining milk in the pot and cook over a low fire, 8 to 10 minutes, stirring constantly, until the mixture thickens. Scrape the vanilla bean pod again, discard the pod, and strain the mixture. Stir in the brandy and butter, then the sliced bananas. Pour into the prepared shell and spread to even the top. You can tap it gently on the counter to level. Cover and chill until firm, about 2 hours.

Just before serving, whip the cream together with the sugar and vanilla extract and spread on top of the pie. Using a potato peeler, peel off chocolate shavings from the bar of chocolate onto waxed or parchment paper. Use a spoon or fork to sprinkle the shavings over the pie. Don't use your hands or the chocolate will melt.

Robert's Silk Pie with Jen's Mocha Variation

Our chef, Robert Cubberly, created the original version of this pie; Jennifer Palmer, our head baker, developed a mocha variation because she and I love mocha. We serve it both ways at the Diner. This pie is full of stuff that's bad for you, so save it for some special occasion. You can make it a day ahead.

MAKES ONE 10-INCH PIE

Hazelnut-Graham Cracker Crust:

¾ cup graham cracker crumbs

¾ cup ground toasted hazelnuts

⅓ cup packed brown sugar

6 tablespoons unsalted butter, melted

Pinch of cinnamon

Pinch of nutmeg

Filling:

1¼ cups unsalted butter

1¼ cups granulated sugar

6 eggs

14 ounces semisweet chocolate, melted and cooled

2 tablespoons espresso powder (optional)

2 tablespoons heavy cream

½ teaspoon vanilla extract

1 cup Chocolate Sauce (page 176)

1 cup heavy cream, whipped

Mix all the crust ingredients together in a mixing bowl until thoroughly combined. Press into the bottom of a 10-inch springform pan. Keep refrigerated while preparing the filling.

In a mixer, cream the butter and sugar together at medium speed until very light and fluffy. Add 3 of the eggs, one by one, beating constantly. Continue beating and add one-quarter of the chocolate and then the remaining eggs, one at a time. Stir in the remaining chocolate. To make the mocha variation, dissolve the espresso powder in the cream, then add it and the vanilla to the filling and beat well. Otherwise, just beat in the cream and vanilla. Pour the mixture onto the crust and chill until firm, at least 3 hours. Overnight is fine.

Remove the springform pan ring and smooth the top and edges. Spread warm Chocolate Sauce over the top and sides. Chill again to set the coating. Serve with a dollop of whipped cream.

Tom's Butterscotch Pudding Pie

This dessert originated with one of our waiters at Mustards Grill
in Napa Valley. Tom liked to make desserts in his spare time (he later left
to open his own cookie company), and he'd regularly bring in
recipes for us to try. The final version of the pudding evolved after a
process of experimentation and fine-tuning, and ended up in a
pie shell. We serve this as a special now and then.

MAKES ONE 9-INCH PIE

1	9-inch Chocolate-Coated Pie Crust (page 203)
3	egg yolks
½	cup unsalted butter
1¼	cups dark brown sugar
1	cup hot water
3	tablespoons cornstarch
2	tablespoons flour
½	teaspoon kosher or sea salt
1⅔	cups milk
2	teaspoons vanilla extract
1½	cups heavy cream
2	tablespoons granulated sugar
½	teaspoon vanilla extract
½	cup Chocolate Sauce (page 176)
½	cup Butterscotch Sauce (recipe follows)
	Powdered sugar

Prepare the pie shell and chill it in the refrigerator.

Beat the egg yolks in a small bowl and set aside. Melt the butter in a saucepan over medium heat and cook until lightly browned. Add the brown sugar and cook, stirring, for about 3 minutes. Stir in the hot water, being careful not to splatter yourself, and remove from the heat.

Combine the cornstarch, flour, and salt in a medium-sized bowl and gradually stir in the milk. Stir this into the butter mixture in the saucepan and return to low heat. Bring to a boil, stirring constantly, and cook for 5 minutes. Whisk about one-fourth of the hot mixture into the egg yolks and then add this back into the remaining mixture in the saucepan. Continue to cook for 1 to 2 minutes, until very thick. Remove from the heat, strain, and stir in 2 teaspoons vanilla. Pour into the chilled pie shell, cover, and chill well.

Combine the heavy cream, granulated sugar, and ½ teaspoon vanilla and whip to soft peaks. Completely cover the pie with the cream. To serve, drizzle a tablespoon of warmed Chocolate Sauce and a tablespoon of warmed Butterscotch Sauce over each portion, and dust with powdered sugar.

Butterscotch Sauce

This sauce keeps indefinitely— just store it in a jar in the refrigerator. My husband, who is a Scot, points out that this sauce has nothing to do with Scotland as far as he knows.

5	tablespoons unsalted butter
¾	cup light brown sugar
¾	cup dark brown sugar
1	cup light corn syrup
1	cup heavy cream

Combine the butter, sugars, and corn syrup in a saucepan and bring to a rolling boil—it should get a little darker as it cooks. Stir in the cream, return to a boil, and then remove pan from heat. This is best served warm.

Caramel Nut Tart

A candy bar in a pie shell. If you serve it with ice cream, the temperature contrast will make it seem less rich. Occasionally we add finely chopped dried apricots and currants to the filling. One large tart could serve up to 12 people easily. You only need very small wedges.

MAKES ONE 11-INCH TART OR TWO 9-INCH TARTS

Tart Shell:

1¼	cups flour
1	tablespoon sugar
¼	teaspoon salt
½	cup plus 2 tablespoons unsalted butter, softened
½	teaspoon vanilla extract
4	teaspoons water

Filling:

2	cups sugar
1	cup water
½	teaspoon lemon juice
⅓	cup heavy cream
½	cup plus 2 tablespoons unsalted butter
1	cup hazelnuts
1	cup almonds
1	cup walnuts
1	cup chopped dried apricots (optional)
¼	cup currants (optional)

To prepare the tart shell, combine the dry ingredients in a bowl and cut in the butter until the mixture is in pea-sized pieces. Add the vanilla and water and mix until the dough comes together. Wrap in plastic and chill for 20 to 30 minutes.

Preheat oven to 350 degrees. Roll out the dough on a lightly floured surface and fit it into the tart pan. Line the shell with foil and fill with pie weights or dried beans. Chill in the refrigerator again for 20 minutes. Bake in the preheated oven for 15 minutes or until golden brown. Remove the foil and pie weights and bake for another 5 minutes.

To prepare the filling, place the sugar, water, and lemon juice in a saucepan, bring to a boil, and cook over medium-high heat to a rich caramel color, stirring all the while. This may take 10 to 15 minutes. Remove from heat and add the cream and butter, being careful that the hot caramel doesn't splatter and bubble over. Transfer to another container to cool slightly.

Toast the nuts separately, as each kind needs a different amount of time (hazelnuts take the longest, walnuts the least). Rub the hazelnuts in a towel to remove excess skin. Don't worry if some of the skin sticks. Allow the nuts to cool, then combine and roughly chop. Combine the nuts and the

apricots and currants at this point for the fruit-and-nut variation.

Place the nuts in the prebaked tart shell and pour the caramel mixture over the top. Bake for 15 minutes in a 350-degree oven, or just until it starts to bubble around the edges.

Allow the tart to cool to room temperature. To serve, cut the pie in wedges. You may want to serve with a scoop of vanilla ice cream and, if you really want to go nuts, add some warmed Chocolate Sauce (page176).

Vanilla Caramel Custard

To get a custard with a true vanilla flavor, I use vanilla beans
rather than vanilla extract, scraping the tiny seeds into the half-and-half.
Your guests may think you're serving them a custard with dirt in it,
so save a bean to show them what the seeds look like.
This custard is an elegant way to end a fine meal.

SERVES 6

Caramel:

½   cup sugar
2   tablespoons light corn syrup
½   cup water

Custard:

½   cup sugar
3   whole eggs plus 3 egg yolks
2½   cups half-and-half
½   vanilla bean

Preheat oven to 325 degrees. Heat water for a water bath: a teakettle works best, as you'll find it easier to pour in the water without splashing any on the custards.

To prepare the caramel, combine the sugar, corn syrup, and water in a saucepan over medium heat. Stir to melt the sugar, and continue to cook, stirring constantly, until the syrup becomes a rich caramel color, about 2 to 3 minutes. Pour a little syrup into 3½-inch ramekins (about 1½ tablespoons or a ¼-inch layer in each). Set aside to cool and harden.

To prepare the custard, beat the sugar with the eggs and egg yolks in a mixing bowl. Put the half-and-half in a saucepan. Split the vanilla bean pod in half lengthwise, scrape the seeds into the saucepan, and drop the pod in, too. Heat until hot but not boiling. Remove the bean pod, scrape it a second time, and discard. Gently whisk the half-and-half into the eggs and mix thoroughly, but not enough to create foam. Strain.

Pour the custard into the ramekins on top of the cooled caramel. Place the ramekins in a water bath (water should come halfway up the sides of the ramekins) and cover the pan with foil. Bake for 30 to 40 minutes, until the custard no longer shakes and an inserted knife comes out clean.

Brûlée refers to a burnt sugar coating, usually on a rich custard.
At the Diner, we caramelize the sugar with a blow torch—it sounds pretty
drastic, but it's the easiest way to get the job done. At home, you
can brown the custards under the broiler, but a blow torch really works best.
I've liked the combination of cardamom and orange ever since
I learned about it from Lois Lee, my first cooking teacher. I think she uses
it in her whole wheat bread. The pieces of chocolate in the
custard add a mouth-watering surprise. In this recipe, I steep the vanilla,
cardamom, and orange zest in the cream for the best flavor.

SERVES 4

2	cups heavy cream
1	teaspoon grated orange zest
1	2-inch piece of vanilla bean
2	cardamom pods
¼	cup sugar
4	egg yolks
1	ounce semisweet chocolate pieces
8	teaspoons sugar

Preheat oven to 325 degrees. Heat water for the water bath.

In a medium-sized saucepan, combine the cream and orange zest. Split the vanilla bean pod in half lengthwise, scrape the seeds into the saucepan, and drop the pod in, too. Remove the cardamom seeds from the pods, roughly chop the seeds, and add them to the cream. Bring just to a boil. Remove from heat and let stand 20 minutes. Remove the bean pod, scrape it a second time, and discard. In a medium-sized bowl, whisk together the sugar and yolks until light and fluffy. Slowly whisk in the warm cream mixture and strain through a fine mesh sieve. Ladle into 3½-inch ceramic ramekins and set in a water bath (the water should reach two-thirds of the way up the ramekins). Cover with foil and cut 6 slits to allow air to escape. Bake for 45 minutes or until just set. Remove custards from water bath. While hot, poke the chocolate pieces into the custards. Cool completely.

To serve, sprinkle 2 teaspoons of sugar on each ramekin and brown the sugar with a blow torch, or place the ramekins under a broiler until the sugar is caramelized.

Tapioca Pudding with Fresh Fruit

I always associate tapioca pudding with my mother, as it was one of the desserts she served us when I was a kid. Any fresh ripe fruit tastes great with tapioca pudding, but blueberries and peaches are especially good. Very lightly sugar the fruit (peel and slice the peaches first). Another possibility is to use the fruit mixture from the Mixed Berry Parfait (page 201).

SERVES 4 TO 6

⅓	cup quick-cooking tapioca
¾	cup sugar
	Pinch of kosher or sea salt
2	eggs, beaten
3½	cups milk
1	vanilla bean
	Fresh fruit, lightly sugared

Put the tapioca, sugar, salt, eggs, and milk in the top of a double boiler. Split the vanilla bean pod in half lengthwise, scrape the seeds into the saucepan, and drop the pod in, too. Gently stir together all the ingredients until thoroughly mixed; do not create a foam. Cook, stirring occasionally for the first 7 minutes or so, then stir constantly for another 8 to 10 minutes, until the mixture thickens enough to coat the back of the spoon. Remove the bean pod, scrape it a second time, and discard. Cool completely. If left uncovered, the pudding will form a skin on top. The skin is like the lumps in mashed potatoes— some people like it, and some don't. If you want to eliminate the skin, cover the surface of the pudding with plastic wrap (the plastic film should actually touch the pudding). Do this when the pudding is still hot.

Ten-Dollar Banana Split

To make a banana split that's really worth $10, you must have
fresh homemade sauces, GREAT vanilla ice cream, and RIPE bananas.
And those split dishes help a lot. When strawberries are not
in season, we use the Jamaican Hot Buttered Rum Sauce and garnish
with toasted coconut. All the sauce recipes follow below.

SERVES 4

4   bananas, peeled and split in
     half lengthwise
12   large scoops vanilla ice cream
½-¾ cup Chocolate Sauce (see
     page 176)
½-¾ cup Pineapple Sauce (recipe
     follows)
½-¾ cup Strawberry Sauce or
     Jamaican Hot Buttered Rum
     Sauce (recipes follow)
½   cup heavy cream, whipped
4   maraschino cherries

Preferably using banana split
dishes, lay the banana halves
lengthwise on the dishes. Arrange
3 scoops of ice cream over the
bananas, one on each end, and
one in the middle. Top each scoop
of ice cream with 2 tablespoons of
each of the three sauces. Top the
middle scoop with a dollop of
whipped cream and a maraschino
cherry.

Pineapple Sauce

How do you tell if a pineapple's
ripe? A Hawaiian friend of mine
would always pull out a leaf—
if it came out easily the pineapple
was ready.

½   fresh pineapple, peeled and
     cored
     Sugar to taste

Purée the pineapple in a processor or blender and add enough
sugar to sweeten the sauce.

Strawberry Sauce

1   pint strawberries, hulled
⅓   cup sugar
     Juice of ½ lemon
2   tablespoons kirsch or triple sec

Place half the strawberries and
the sugar and lemon juice in a
blender or processor, and purée.
Strain into a serving bowl. Slice
the remaining strawberries,
and mix with the purée, together
with the kirsch or triple sec.

Jamaican Hot Buttered Rum Sauce

This sauce got its name from the
Jamaican-made Myers's rum that
goes into. You don't have to use
Myers's, but you do need a dark
rum in order to get the right
appearance and flavor.

½   cup sugar
¼   cup water
¼   cup light corn syrup
3   tablespoons Myers's dark rum
⅓   cup heavy cream
¼   teaspoon grated nutmeg
1   tablespoon unsalted butter

Combine the sugar, water, and
syrup in a saucepan and bring to
a boil. Reduce heat and simmer
until a caramel forms. Remove
pan from heat and slowly add the
remaining ingredients, being
careful not to burn yourself on the
steam and liquid boiling up in the
pan. Stir well to incorporate,
return to the heat, and cook until
the mixture is completely melted
and smooth, about 3 minutes.

T—Sundae

We named this sundae after a certain candy that it vaguely resembled
until some big shot conglomerate sent their lawyers after us,
and said they had trademarked the name and we couldn't use it. So now the sundae
is not even on the menu, but we still get a million requests
for it and we serve it under this alias. Needless to say, I quit buying this
company's products. I always hate being told what to do.

SERVES 4

½ cup Chocolate Sauce (page 176)
2 cups seasoned pecans
   (page 228)
8 scoops vanilla ice cream
½ cup Butterscotch Sauce
   (page 192)
⅓ cup whipped cream

Pour 1 tablespoon of Chocolate
Sauce into each parfait or sundae
glass and place 3 or 4 pecans
and a scoop of ice cream on top.
Pour a tablespoon of Butterscotch
Sauce on the ice cream and 3 or 4
more pecans. Add another scoop
of ice cream, followed by a tablespoon each of the Chocolate
and Butterscotch Sauces, whipped
cream, and 2 or 3 pecans.

Gingersnap Cookies

These are great dunked into an espresso or a cup of tea. If you prefer a crispier cookie you can substitute vegetable shortening for the butter.

	Butter for cookie sheets
¾	cup butter
1	cup sugar
1	egg
¼	cup molasses
2	tablespoons grated fresh ginger
2	cups flour
2	teaspoons baking soda
½	teaspoon salt
1	teaspoon cinnamon
	Extra sugar

Preheat oven to 350 degrees and butter cookie sheets, or line them with parchment paper.

In a mixing bowl, cream together the butter and sugar. Add the egg, and beat until light and fluffy, then beat in the molasses and ginger. In a separate bowl combine the flour, baking soda, salt, and cinnamon. Add to the first mixture, beating until smooth and blended.

Pinch off small pieces of dough and roll them into 1-inch balls, using the palms of your hands. Roll the balls in a little extra sugar and place about 2 inches apart on the cookie sheet. Bake for 10 to 12 minutes, until they have spread and the tops begin to crack. Cool on a rack.

Mixed Berry Parfait with Gingersnaps

This parfait is a great made with summer fruit, but you can use other kinds of fruit, depending on what's in season and what has the best flavor at the time.

Fruit:

½	cup blueberries
½	cup blackberries
½	cup strawberries, stemmed and quartered
1	cup peaches, apricots, or nectarines, peeled and sliced
2	teaspoons fresh lemon juice
1-2	tablespoons powdered sugar
1	teaspoon vanilla extract
	Splash of triple sec, Grand Marnier, or other liqueur of your choice (optional)

12	large scoops (1 quart) vanilla ice cream
½	cup whipped cream
6-12	Gingersnap Cookies (see preceding recipe)

In a large mixing bowl, gently mix the fruits, lemon juice, sugar, vanilla, and optional liqueur. Refrigerate until ready to serve. It's best if the mixture can macerate for 30 minutes.

For each serving, place 2 tablespoons of the fruit mixture in the bottom of a parfait glass or large malt glass. Add 1 scoop of ice cream, 4 tablespoons of fruit, another scoop of ice cream, and more fruit. Top with a dollop of whipped cream and serve 1 or 2 gingersnaps on the side.

Peanut Butter Chocolate Chip Cookies

MAKES 4 DOZEN COOKIES

My stepson Peter likes these. He once ate 20 of
them on the drive to a snow-boarding weekend.
This was quite a feat because these cookies are
big. We use them to make ice cream sandwiches
(see next recipe).

2	cups unsalted butter
1½	cups granulated sugar
1½	cups dark brown sugar
2	teaspoons kosher or sea salt
4	eggs
2	teaspoons vanilla extract
¼	cup water
2	cups unsalted peanut butter
4	cups flour
2	teaspoons baking soda
2	cups chocolate chips

Preheat the oven to 350 degrees.

Cream together the butter, sugars, and salt.
Add the eggs one at a time, beating well after each.
Blend in the vanilla, water, and peanut butter; incorporate thoroughly but do not overmix. Stir in the
flour and baking soda until just mixed, and fold
in the chocolate chips.

If you want giant cookies that will hold four
scoops of ice cream, use an ice cream scoop to measure out the dough. Drop the dough onto a cookie
sheet lined with parchment paper, allowing 4 inches
between the cookies, as the dough will spread quite
a bit. For smaller cookies (the right size for one
healthy scoop of ice cream), 2 tablespoons of dough
is about right, and space the cookies about 2 inches
apart. Bake for 8 to 12 minutes, or until lightly
browned and crisp at the edges.

Peanut Butter Cookie Ice Cream Sandwich

SERVES 2

There are so many ways to do these. Depending
on how large you make the cookie, the ice cream
sandwich can hold from one to four scoops of ice
cream. It would probably be less intimidating to
make the cookies the size of one scoop of ice cream
and then give each person two sandwiches, one of
each flavor. We make them big enough for two
people at the Diner, using two large cookies and
four scoops of ice cream.

2	Peanut Butter Chocolate Chip Cookies (see preceding recipe)
2	scoops vanilla ice cream
2	scoops chocolate ice cream
¼	cup Chocolate Sauce (page 176)
	Whipped cream
	Toasted Spanish peanuts
	Powdered sugar

Place 1 cookie on a serving plate, put 1 scoop each
of vanilla and chocolate ice cream on the cookie,
top with another cookie, and drizzle with 2 tablespoons Chocolate Sauce. Add a dollop of whipped
cream, sprinkle with peanuts, and dust with
powdered sugar.

Basic Pie Crust

You can use this crust for just about any kind of pie.
Directions are included for prebaking the pie shell.

MAKES TWO 9-INCH CRUSTS

2   cups flour
¾   teaspoon salt
1½   teaspoons sugar
1   cup plus 2 tablespoons
      unsalted butter, cold and diced
3   tablespoons ice water

In a medium bowl, combine the
flour, salt, and sugar. Cut the butter
into the flour until the mixture is
the size of small peas. Sprinkle ice
water over the top and mix lightly
until the dough comes together.
Press the dough into a disk, cover
it with plastic wrap, and chill
for 30 minutes.

On a lightly floured surface, roll
the dough out ⅛ to ¼ inch thick.
Fit it into pans, flute the edges, and
chill again until firm.

If the recipe calls for a baked
shell, prick the bottom of the crust
4 or 5 times with a fork and line
the chilled dough with foil, press-
ing firmly into the corners of the

pie. Fill with pie weights (these can
be purchased at most stores that
handle cookware) or dried beans.
Bake in a 375-degree oven for
20 to 30 minutes or until the crust
is set and lightly browned all over.
Remove the foil and pie weights
and bake for another 5 minutes.

Chocolate-Coated Pie Crust

If you want to line the crust
with chocolate, bake the crust as
directed above, and sprinkle it
with 2 ounces of grated semisweet
chocolate right after you take it
out of the oven. Let it stand a few
minutes, then spread the chocolate
with the back of a spoon, covering
the bottom and sides.
Chill until the
chocolate is set.

BEVE[R...]
CHAP[...]

RAGES

TER 9

BEVERAGES

Drinks, both alcoholic and nonalcoholic, are a big part of the Diner's spirit. After all, you can't have a burger without a malt or a shake, and what's a Sunday brunch without a Bloody Mary? It was Boo who set the ambience and style of the bar. In doing this, he got plenty of input from Doug Biederbeck, who was our opening general manager and is now our partner at Bix, and from Joe Peck, who started as assistant manager and is now the general manager of the Diner. The bar is sophisticated, but unintimidating; and fun without being silly. There are only a few rules—like no blender drinks—and the Bloody Mary must be served up, not on the rocks, and not overwhelmed by a celery stick the size of a California redwood. We use the best liquor available, and our selection has grown to include over 16 single malt Scotch whiskies and vodkas in every flavor under the sun. Our wine list is solid, too.   Many of our drinks were created in response to our customers' requests for something fun or new and different. This is especially true of our selection of non-alcoholic drinks. All the recipes that follow are for a single drink: multiply quantities as needed.

Barbados Cosmos

A delightfully refreshing cocktail—not found in
Barbados, however, but right here in San Francisco!

1½   ounces Mount Gay rum (Eclipse)
      Juice of ½ lime
      Dash each of cranberry juice and Simple Syrup
      (page 214)

Place ingredients in a cocktail shaker with ice and
shake well. Serve up in a stemmed 3-ounce cocktail
glass.

Picon Punch

As far as I know, this cocktail was invented in
San Francisco. It's made with Amer Picon, a very
aromatic, orange-flavored apéritif wine. A good
drink for brunches.

      Grenadine syrup
1   scoop ice
1½   ounces Amer Picon
      Splash of soda water
      Brandy (Armagnac if you have it)

Lightly coat a 7-ounce short-stemmed cocktail glass
with grenadine, and pour out and shake off excess.
Fill the glass with ice, and pour in the Amer Picon
and enough soda to just about reach the rim. Add a
float of brandy and serve with a twist of lemon.

Diner Manhattan

This is our downtown version of the classic
Manhattan. Instead of sweet vermouth, we use
St. Raphael, a wine-based apéritif that is fortified
with additional spirits. St. Raphael is mildly
bitter.

1½   ounces Wild Turkey bourbon
½   ounce St. Raphael (or Dubonnet)
      Dash of Angostura bitters

Place ingredients in a cocktail shaker with ice and
shake well. Strain into a stemmed 3-ounce cocktail
glass. Garnish with a maraschino cherry.

Billy Burger's Pterodactyl

Billy Burger is one of our bartenders extraordinaire.
He has two passions in life: mixing drinks and
making neon pterodactyls, which is how this drink
got its name. One Friday night a customer said,
"Make us a green drink," and here it is.

1½   ounces Stolichnaya Limonnaya vodka
      Juice of ½ lime
      Splash of Simple Syrup (page 214)
      Splash of pineapple juice

Place ingredients in a cocktail shaker with ice and
shake well. Strain into a 3-ounce stemmed cocktail
glass.

Rasputin

We once held a contest among the staff to see who could invent the best drink using Stoli Cristall. This was the winner—invented by Roger Nissim, our opening bartender. It's named after a character in a novel that Roger was reading at the time.

1   scoop ice
1½   ounces Stolichnaya Cristall vodka
     Dash of framboise (raspberry brandy)

Place ingredients in a cocktail shaker and shake well. Strain into a chilled 3-ounce long-stemmed cocktail glass and serve garnished with a twist of lemon.

Fog City Diner Lemonade

Very refreshing. For a lemonade that packs a punch, add 1½ ounces of Stolichnaya vodka.

2   ounces fresh lemon juice
     Soda water to fill glass
     Simple Syrup (page 214), to taste

Combine the above ingredients and serve over ice in a 12-ounce water glass. Garnish with a wedge of lemon.

Bloody Mary

We make a traditional Bloody Mary, shaken over ice, and served "up" without a salad bar of additives. One of these, together with two aspirins, a burger, and a malt, is just what the doctor ordered for those Saturday morning hangovers.

1½   ounces vodka
     Juice of ½ lemon or more
     Pinch of freshly ground black pepper
4-5 dashes Worcestershire sauce
4-5 ounces tomato juice
     Dash of salt

Place ingredients in a cocktail shaker filled with ice and shake well. Serve in a 6- to 7-ounce glass and garnish with a slice of lemon.

Lime Rickey

One of our most popular and refreshing nonalcoholic "cocktails." If you can't find the Sweet and Sour, use our lemonade (see recipe above).

1   ounce Rose's lime juice
3   ounces G. Grecos's Sweet and Sour
3   ounces Sprite or 7Up
3   ounces soda water
     Juice of ½ lime

Combine all the liquid ingredients, shake, and serve over ice in a 12-ounce water glass. Garnish with half a lime.

Bay Breeze

Our nonalcoholic answer to the sea breeze, soon to be a San Francisco classic—and Fog City's remedy for the common cold.

4	ounces cranberry juice
4	ounces freshly squeezed grapefruit juice

Combine the ingredients and serve in a 12-ounce water glass over ice.

Hot Apple Pie

A great warmer-upper, especially after a day of skiing or mushroom hunting. Also makes a good after-dinner drink. Serve it instead of dessert.

1½	ounces Tuaca
	Apple cider to fill glass
1	stick cinnamon
	Whipped cream

Heat a 6- to 7-ounce short-stemmed cocktail glass by filling it with hot water. Pour out the water and pour in the Tuaca and cider. Garnish with the cinnamon stick and top with whipped cream.

Hot Chocolate Mint

This cocktail is both a beverage and a dessert. If you can't get the powdered chocolate, you could sift a little powdered sugar and a little cocoa together to get something similar. If you have an espresso maker, use steamed milk.

1½	ounces Rumpleminz
1	ounce Chocolate Sauce (page 176)
	Hot milk to fill glass
	Sprinkle of Ghirardelli's powdered chocolate

Put the first three ingredients in a 12-ounce water glass and sprinkle with powdered chocolate.

Hot Toddy

This is great on a cold and foggy San Francisco summer night.

1	lump sugar
1½	ounces rye whisky or bourbon
	Boiling water to fill glass
1	stick cinnamon
3-4	cloves
2	slices lemon

Heat a 6- to 7-ounce short-stemmed glass by filling it with hot water. Discard the water. Put in the sugar and whisky, and add boiling water to fill the glass. Garnish with the cinnamon stick, cloves, and slices of lemon.

Hot Buttered Rum

Even summer evenings are cold in San Francisco, so you could call this a drink for all seasons here. Throughout the years this has been our most popular drink.

1½ ounces Myers's Rum
1 tablespoon Hot Buttered Rum Mix (see below)
  Boiling water to fill glass
1 stick cinnamon
1 roaring fire (optional)

Heat a 6- to 7-ounce short-stemmed cocktail glass by filling it with hot water. Pour out the water, pour in the rum, add the Rum Mix, and pour in boiling water to fill. Garnish with a cinnamon stick. Best served by the (optional) roaring fire.

Hot Buttered Rum Mix

4 tablespoons dark brown sugar
2 tablespoons light brown sugar
½ cup butter
  Pinch of nutmeg
  Pinch of cinnamon
  Pinch of cloves
  Zest of ½ lemon
  Zest of ½ orange

Mix all ingredients together and keep chilled.

Hot Milk Punch

We gave this old-fashioned New Orleans punch a couple of new twists. This is a good one to serve for brunch.

1 tablespoon sugar
¼ ounce rum
¾ ounce brandy
  Hot milk to fill glass
  Dash of nutmeg

Heat a 12-ounce water glass by filling it with hot water. Discard the water and add the ingredients as listed above.

Vanilla Shake

This recipe is dedicated to Tyler Higgins, my partner's son. Tyler drinks 250 to 300 of these a year as he makes the rounds of our restaurants with his father. According to him, Fog City Diner's is the best!

3   scoops vanilla ice cream
¼   cup milk

Combine the ingredients in a blender and blend. Serve in a 12-ounce glass.

Variations:

For a Chocolate Shake, use a touch less milk and blend in ¼ cup of Chocolate Sauce (page 176).

For a Strawberry Shake, blend in about 3 ounces of strawberries.

For a Malted Shake—vanilla, chocolate, or strawberry—just add 2 mounded tablespoons malt to the other ingredients before blending.

Simple Syrup

This sugar syrup is used in several of our drinks. It keeps well refrigerated, so I often make a double batch and keep it in a bottle in the refrigerator. In Japan they use a similar syrup to sweeten chilled teas. It's a great idea because it's already dissolved and you use less.

1   cup sugar
1   cup water

Combine the ingredients in a medium saucepan and bring to a full rolling boil. Simmer for 5 minutes. Cool before using.

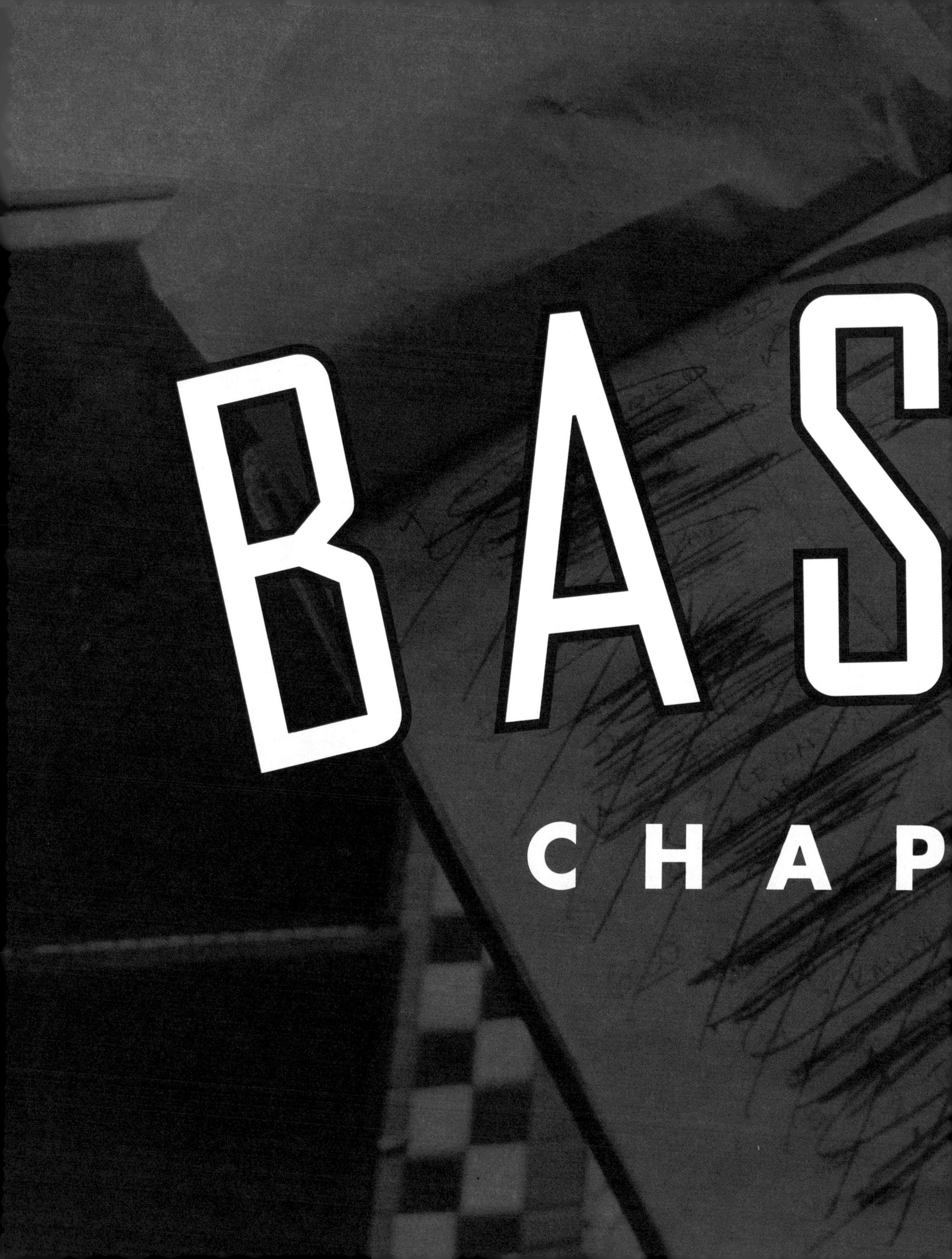

BAS

CHAP

BASICS

I've included in this chapter

recipes for such

basic provisions as stocks and

spice blends.

You'll find that preparing

meals is so much

easier if you have these

items on hand,

especially those that you find

yourself using frequently.

Following the recipes

are some general hints on

food preparation.

Veal Stock

To make a good stock, it is very important to use plenty of meaty bones and
fresh vegetables: scraps make good compost and that's about it.
For the best flavor, use some shank bones that have some meat attached to them.
Always start with cold water and skim often to keep the broth clear.
You can make either a light stock or a dark stock (see directions below).

YIELDS 3 QUARTS

10	pounds veal bones
1	pound onions, diced
6	cloves garlic
¼	pound celery, diced
½	pound carrots, diced
½	pound turnips, rutabagas, or parsnips, diced
6	sprigs thyme
6	sprigs parsley
1	tablespoon black peppercorns
2	bay leaves
8-10	quarts cold water

For a light stock, place the bones and vegetables in a stockpot and add enough water to cover. Bring the water to a full rolling boil and skim off any foam and fat that comes to the surface. Reduce heat to a gentle simmer and add the spices and herbs. Simmer, skimming often, for 3 to 5 hours. Strain and cool thoroughly, then degrease.

For a rich dark stock, begin by roasting the bones and pieces of meat to a dark golden brown (set them in a roasting pan in a 400-degree oven), add the onions with the skins on and the diced vegetables and continue to roast until the vegetables are very dark. Pour off the fat that has been rendered and deglaze the roasting pan. Continue as for the light stock, adding the juices from the pan.

Beef Stock

Follow the directions above for Veal Stock, using beef bones instead. Beef Stock can also be made light or dark.

Chicken Stock

YIELDS 3 QUARTS

As for any stock, you must start with fresh ingredients, handle them carefully, and skim the stock often. For a dark stock, roast the bones and the onions before beginning (see directions for Veal Stock).

2½-3 pounds chicken bones
3   stalks celery, diced
2   pounds onions, diced
6   cloves garlic
1   turnip, diced
1   rutabaga, diced
1   parsnip, diced
4-5 quarts cold water
2   bay leaves
2   teaspoons peppercorns, cracked
1   teaspoon coriander seeds
2   whole cloves
3   sprigs thyme
6   sprigs parsley
2   teaspoons allspice

Place the bones and vegetables in a stockpot and add water to cover. Bring to a boil and reduce heat to a simmer, skimming off the fats and solids that rise to the top. Add the herbs and spices, and continue simmering for 2 hours, skimming off the top as needed. Strain, cool, and degrease the stock.

Fish Stock

YIELDS 3 QUARTS

This is probably the last thing a home cook would want to make or could find the ingredients for. But if, by chance, you do find yourself with 3 pounds of bones from a halibut, or a monkfish, or some sole, don't let them go to waste. This stock makes an excellent base for chowders, or for steaming fresh clams or mussels. Those who are not so fortunate as to have fish stock on hand can make do with chicken stock, vegetable stock, or just plain water.

3   pounds white fish bones (not salmon or tuna)
2   tablespoons olive oil
2   large onions, peeled and diced
1   bulb fennel, diced
2   leeks, white parts only, diced
3   stalks celery, diced
1   shallot, peeled
3   cloves garlic
1   quart white wine
3   quarts cold water
1   bay leaf
6   sprigs thyme
1   teaspoon white peppercorns, smashed
6   sprigs Italian parsley
2   teaspoon cracked coriander seeds

Rinse the fish bones. Heat the olive oil in a large pot, add the fish bones, and cook, stirring, until the bones become opaque. Do not brown them. Add the onions, fennel, leeks, celery, shallot, and garlic, stir to coat with oil, and cook 2 minutes, again without browning. Add the wine and bring to a boil. Add the water and return just to the boil. Reduce heat to a bare simmer, add the remaining ingredients, and simmer 1½ hours. Skim often. When done strain, cool, and degrease.

Vegetable Stock

Always keep some of this on hand—it's a quick and easy way to add flavor to soups, stews, and sauces. Make sure you use fresh vegetables: trim off the root ends and excess greens to avoid bitterness.

2	onions, peeled and chopped
2	leeks, white parts only, chopped
4	carrots, peeled and chopped
3-4	stalks celery, chopped
1-2	bulbs fennel, chopped
1-2	bulbs celery root (optional)
2-3	ripe tomatoes or 2 cups tomato juice
2	parsnips, peeled and chopped
2	turnips, peeled and chopped
2	rutabagas, peeled and chopped
4	quarts water
2	bay leaves
1	bunch parsley, stems only
½	bunch thyme
¼	bunch mint
1	tablespoon black peppercorns
2	tablespoons whole coriander seeds

Bring all the vegetables to a boil in the water. Reduce to a simmer and skim off any foam that rises to the top. Add the herbs and spices and simmer for 1½ hours. Strain and cool.

Court Bouillon

Use this flavored broth for cooking shrimp, crab, and lobster.

2	quarts water
6	tablespoons kosher or sea salt
12	bay leaves
	Juice of 6 lemons
2	tablespoons mustard seeds
2	tablespoons peppercorns
2	bottles beer
2	tablespoons chile flakes
2	tablespoons cayenne

Combine all the ingredients in a pot large enough to hold the crabs, shrimp, or lobsters you intend to cook. Bring to a boil and boil 5 minutes before adding the shellfish. Depending on the size, prawns will take 1 to 3 minutes and a 2-pound lobster will take 7 to 8 minutes. For crabs, I usually figure on 7 minutes per pound.

Vinegar

There is a wide variety of vinegars available in the markets today. You can find wine vinegars, malt vinegars, rice vinegars, and vinegars flavored with berries, fruits, or herbs, each with its own distinct flavor and level of tartness. Red wine and champagne vinegars are aged in wood and have a slight sharpness. Aged sherry vinegar has a mellow wood-aged flavor, and balsamic vinegar has a natural sweetness and richness. Probably the best vinegar of all is one you make at home from leftover red wine. For more information on making your own vinegar, consult Richard Olney's *Simple French Food*.

I can't stress enough how important good vinegar is to the final flavor of a dish.

Herbs

In California we are fortunate to have most fresh herbs available all year round. We take advantage of this good fortune at the Diner and use fresh herbs exclusively, so when herbs are called for in the recipes here, that means fresh herbs. I haven't used dried herbs in years, so if that is what you prefer to cook with or all you have available, you'll need to experiment with the amounts needed. You might start with one-fourth to one-half as much dried as fresh. Start with less, as you can always add more later.

For the home cook, the best of all possible worlds would be to have herbs growing right in your garden so you can pick them as needed for cooking. That's really fresh!

Spices

I've always preferred to buy spices whole and grind them myself: you can always tell the difference when it comes down to the taste. The flavor of freshly ground spices is so great that it's worth it to invest in a spice mill or a small electric grinder. Try to get one with a clear top so you can check the fineness of the grind. I use a coffee bean grinder for grinding spices. If you want to do this, get one just for spices, preferably in a different color from the one you use to grind your coffee beans. Always dust out the mill or grinder thoroughly after each use so the next spice you grind won't be contaminated by the last one. A little cayenne in your cinnamon would be detrimental to your apple pie. If you're patient, use a mortar and pestle for grinding up spices.

I like to toast whole spices such as cumin seeds, sesame seeds, or coriander seeds before grinding them because this brings out more of the spice flavor. I sometimes toast such spice mixtures as curry and chile powders for the same reason. Toasting is best done in a dry skillet over medium-high heat. Shake the pan constantly until the desired aroma has developed, usually 1½ to 2 minutes at most. Taking this extra step will improve the taste of the finished dish tenfold.

BBQ Pork Spice Blend

This is more than you'd need for one round of barbecued pork, but it will keep for a bit, and it's nice to have on hand for other dishes. It's good sprinkled on grilled chicken, fish, or lamb.

2	teaspoons cumin seeds
½	cup chile powder
2	teaspoons curry powder
2	cloves garlic, minced
1½	teaspoons cayenne
2	teaspoons salt
3	tablespoons paprika
3	tablespoons freshly ground white pepper

Toast the cumin seeds and grind them in a mortar and pestle or spice mill. Toast the chile and curry powders in a dry skillet, and combine all the ingredients.

Chile Paste

You can vary the chiles in this recipe depending on your preference and the availability in your area. This is the combination we use.

2	dried ancho or cascabel chiles
2	dried pasilla negro chiles
2	dried guajillo chiles

Preheat oven to 350 degrees. Stem and seed the chiles. Place them on a cookie sheet or roasting pan, and toast 5 to 8 minutes, until the aroma of the chiles develops.

Put the chiles in a medium-sized bowl, add hot water to cover, and soak until soft. Drain off all but ½ cup of water. Blend the chile and ¼ to ½ cup of the reserved water in a blender until smooth, then rub through a sieve. Store in the refrigerator.

Red or Green Curry Paste

This is a variation of a condiment that is commonly used in Indonesian cooking. This differs from the traditional curry paste because it doesn't contain shrimp paste or dried shrimp. This will make a big batch: you can store it in the refrigerator, or better yet, share it with your friends and neighbors.

YIELDS 4 CUPS

1½	teaspoons coriander seeds
1	teaspoon cumin seeds
1	teaspoon fennel seeds
1	teaspoon black peppercorns
4	whole cloves
20	red serrano, jalapeño, or other chiles
¼	cup olive oil
2	large shallots, peeled and sliced
4	cloves garlic
½	bunch cilantro
1	stalk lemon grass, bottom 4 inches only
1-2	slices fresh ginger, peeled
¼	whole nutmeg, grated
	Zest of ½ lime
1	teaspoon salt

Toast the coriander, cumin, and fennel seeds, peppercorns, and cloves in a dry skillet, shaking often, until you can really smell the aroma. Combine all the ingredients in a processor or blender and blend until smooth.

Note: You can also try different combinations of chiles. Here's one that works well for a slightly milder condiment: 1 red bell pepper, 1 pasilla chile, and 6 to 8 jalapeños.

Croutons

You can't make good croutons without good bread—even day-old good bread will make good croutons.

1   French baguette or Italian loaf
2   tablespoons olive oil

Cut the baguette or Italian loaf on the bias into ¼-inch-thick slices, brush with the olive oil and toast on a baking sheet in a 325-degree oven or under a broiler until golden brown. Don't try to rush this; croutons need to be cooked slowly so they are crisp all the way through.

Often for soup we'll cut or tear the bread into small pieces, mix with oil, salt, and pepper, and bake until crisp. The special croutons for the Caesar Salad (page 109) are seasoned with garlic.

Toasted Nuts

Toasting brings out the full flavor of nuts, so almost without exception, we take this extra step when a recipe calls for nuts of any kind.

Preheat oven to 350 degrees. Spread the nuts on a baking sheet and toast in the oven until lightly browned. Cool before using. With hazelnuts, it is best to rub the skins off in a towel while the nuts are still warm.

Seasoned Nuts

YIELDS 2 CUPS

These are addictive. They make great gifts and have a million different uses. Leftovers, if there are any, should be stored in airtight containers. You can do this with pecans, walnut halves, almonds, hazelnuts, pistachios, or peanuts.

2   cups raw shelled nuts
1   quart water
½-¾ cup powdered sugar
3   cups peanut oil
         Kosher or sea salt

If the nuts have skins that are easily removed, rub off the skins. Place the nuts in a pan with the water and bring to a boil. Remove from heat, drain, and immediately coat thoroughly with powdered sugar. Heat the oil to 375 degrees in a deep-fryer or cast-iron skillet, and fry the nuts until golden and crisp. Do not overcrowd while frying. Drain them on a cookie sheet or in a colander. (Do not drain them on paper towels as they will stick.) While still hot, sprinkle with salt to taste.

Peeling Garlic

I've always hated cleaning out garlic presses so I don't use them. I smash the garlic cloves with the broad side of a cleaver to split the skins, then I simply pull off the skins and mince the garlic.

Peeling Tomatoes

Cut out the stem and make an X on the bottom of the tomato. Drop it into boiling water for 30 seconds to 1 minute, until the skin pulls off easily (the riper it is, the less time it will take). If you're using the tomato raw for a salad, plunge it immediately into ice water to cool it before peeling. If you're going to cook it, just peel and chop.

Grating Ginger

Peel off the thin skin before grating. I use a small bamboo ginger grater that I got in Chinatown. It keeps the stringy fibers on one side and the nicely grated flesh and juice pass through. I've also used the fine holes on a box grater with good results. Before tossing out the fibrous material, squeeze out any remaining juice.

Roasting and Peeling Peppers and Chiles

Many recipes call for roasted peeled peppers or chiles. The easiest way to accomplish this is to brown them under a broiler or right on a gas burner. Get them nice and charred, then stick them in a bowl, and cover the bowl tightly with plastic wrap. Let them steam for 10 minutes, and the skins should just slip off.

Grilling

There are many styles of grills available today—you can get wood or charcoal, gas or electric, indoor or outdoor—everything from portable tabletop models to the fancy ones with automatic ignitors and power rotisseries. In my opinion, the flavor is best off a wood or charcoal fire. For these, it's convenient to have a damper to help control the fire, and some kind of crank so the grill can be moved easily closer to or further away from the fire—both of these features will help you regulate the cooking. You can use a variety of woods for cooking such as mesquite, oak, or almond. The hard woods produce a hotter fire that will burn for a longer time.

Notes on Cooking Fish

To cook fish, rub it first with olive oil and season it with salt and pepper. Sear it on a griddle, or in a cast-iron nonstick sauté pan, or on the grill. The idea of the searing is to seal in the juices and to put a golden crispy crust on the fish. If the fish looks like it might become too brown on the outside before it's cooked on the inside, you can finish the cooking in a preheated 350-degree oven.

It's difficult to determine exact cooking times for you to follow because the thickness of the fillet or steak, the heat of the fire, and the type or density of the flesh all make a difference. Some fish, such as tuna and salmon, can be served medium-rare, while others need to be cooked through. (On no account, though, should any kind of fish be overcooked, as it will become dry and tasteless.) A rule of thumb when using a medium fire is cook the fish fillet about 8 to 10 minutes per inch of thickness. To cook it to medium-rare, you could cut the cooking time in half. If you have a very hot fire, you may also need to cut the cooking time a bit, although it would be best to wait until the coals have calmed down before grilling. At the Diner, we would cook a 6½- to 7-ounce fillet of salmon from a 9- to 12-pound fish for about 2 to 2½ minutes per side.

Have Fun!
982-2000
982-2000
982-2000
PAGEANT MATCH, INC.
G CITY
NER
STREET
NCISCO
UNUSUAL DISHES
UNUSUAL DISHES
1300 BATTERY STREET
SAN FRANCISCO
UNUSUAL DISHES
Have Fun!
Have Fun!

BASMATI RICE   A fragrant long-grain rice from India. It has a wonderful nutlike flavor. Cook it as you would any rice. There are some varieties of basmati rice grown in Texas.

BLACK BEAN PASTE   An oriental condiment made from fermented salted black beans. There are many varieties—some contain hot chiles or garlic, or both. Check the ingredients list before buying to make sure you're getting one that does not contain MSG.

CHIFFONADE   A French cooking term which means fine threads. It is generally used in reference to cutting lettuces and herbs into thin strips like tiny ribbons.

CHILE FLAKES   Usually sold as dried red chile flakes or dried red pepper flakes. It's the same seasoning you see in shakers at pizza parlors.

FISH SAUCE   Used in Vietnamese cooking. Made from fermented salted fish such as anchovies. You could substitute minced anchovies and water.

HOISIN   A thick soybean-based condiment used in Chinese cooking. It is good for marinades and barbecue sauces. Use it with meat and poultry.

KETJAP MANIS   An Indonesian condiment that is similar to soy sauce, but sweeter and thicker. It's available at Asian and specialty markets. You can substitute two parts tamari or dark soy to one part molasses as a substitute.

LEMON GRASS   A common ingredient in Thai cuisine. Has a scallion/onion-like bulb at the base, and a grassy top; has a sour-lemon fragrance and flavor. The leaves are used for teas, and the bulb is finely minced for sauces, marinades, and salads. For cooking, use only the bottom 5 or 6 inches of the bulb end.

SAMBAL OLECK   A condiment used in Indonesian and Malaysian cuisines. It is made with chile peppers and other spices. It is available in Indonesian markets and some specialty stores. You can substitute Chinese-style chile pastes if you wish.

TAMARI   A Japanese soy sauce. Somewhat thicker than Chinese-style soy sauces.

VANILLA BEANS   Come from several different places, but the Tahitian and the Bourbon beans are the easiest to get. To me, the Tahitian bean seems to be more aromatic, while the Bourbon is stronger in flavor. Look for plump, supple pods. In the book *The Artful Eater*, Edward Behr goes into great detail on vanilla, including instructions on making your own extract.

WASABI   A Japanese horseradish, commonly found in the U.S. in powdered form. To use, mix with water to desired consistency.

Here is a list of books that I have read, reread, and continuously turn to for advice, inspiration, and sometimes for a good laugh. I've learned a lot from these books and I know I'll learn more. (I've also included some great reference books for oddball ingredients.) I hope you will enjoy them and find them helpful.

Beard, James. *James Beard's American Cookery*, New York: Little, Brown, & Co., 1980.

Bhumichitr, Vatcharin. *The Taste of Thailand*, New York: Macmillan, 1988.

Child, Julia. *Julia Child & Company*, New York: Alfred A. Knopf, 1978.

Clayton, Bernard, Jr. *The New Complete Book of Breads*, New York: Simon & Schuster, 1987.

Cunningham, Marion. *Fanny Farmer Cookbook, 13th rev. ed.*, New York: Alfred A. Knopf, 1990.

Herbst, Sharon Tyler. *Food Lover's Companion: Comprehensive Definitions of Over 3,000 Food, Wine, and Culinary Terms*, New York: Barron, 1989.

Olney, Richard. *Simple French Food*, New York: Macmillan, 1977.

Rombauer, Irma S. and Becke, Marion Rombauer. *Joy of Cooking*, Bobbs-Merrill Co., Inc., 1975.

Schlesinger, Chris and Willoughby, John. *The Thrill of the Grill: Techniques, Recipes, and Down Home Barbecue*, New York: Morrow, 1990.

Shere, Lindsey. *Chez Panisse Desserts*, New York: Random, 1985.

Silverton, Nancy. *Desserts*, New York: Harper and Row, 1986.

Stern, Jane and Stern, Michael. *A Taste of America*, Andrews and McMeel, 1988.

Time-Life Foods of the World Series, New York: Time-Life Books.

Time-Life Good Cook Series. New York: Time-Life Books.

THE END